THE PAYOFF OF PAIN

HOW TO TURN YOUR PAIN INTO POWER

DANIELLE HARRIS-BRANCH

ISBN: 979-8-89316-028-4 (paperback)
ISBN: 979-8-89316-029-1 (ebook)
ISBN: 979-8-89316-110-6 (hardcover)

DOWNLOAD YOUR FREE GIFT.

To say thanks for buying my book,
I would like to give you my
freedom blueprint 100% FREE!

Visit **daniellehbranch.com/resources**

This book is dedicated to my husband, Delmar Malaik Branch. Thank you for your example, resilience, care, support, wisdom, faith, and most importantly, your love. You changed my life forever. I have been loved perfectly for a lifetime, and for that, I am profoundly grateful. May the ripples of your life continue to mend, uplift, and inspire hope for those in hopeless circumstances.

TABLE OF CONTENTS

INTRODUCTION

It was the winter of 2016 when we received the news that my husband Delmar's kidneys were failing. I felt as if we were being pranked. I'd known his transplant wouldn't last forever, but did it have to be now? If God didn't step in and perform a miracle, our freedom would be coming to an end.

Keeping the faith, we trusted God to deliver Delmar's complete recovery. But things didn't turn out as we expected. I spent so many nights lying in bed, weeping so hard my eyes were swollen shut, fighting off strange migraines that only got worse in the dark. I couldn't bear watching the love of my life suffer. It shattered my heart to powder. Devastated by my circumstances, some days I felt like I had lost myself entirely.

For most of our marriage, Delmar had been in the bed of affliction. Time and time again, we'd fought to save money and make time for our dreams. Still, between surgeries and recovery, medical bills and medications, and collections from the aftermath of medical needs, we often ended up depleted. I just wanted to be free to love and do what ordinary people did. Couldn't we have a beautiful day without any health complications? Take a nice trip without sickness in the driver's seat. Have a romantic evening with plenty of sex... without illness dictating when, how often, and how long. But the sickness didn't ask us what we wanted. It just demanded what it needed. It felt like sickness was the unwelcome third wheel in our relationship.

At times, I would look into my husband's eyes and see his sincere regret for taking me on this journey with him. He would even apologize, which ripped my heart to pieces. I would quickly reply, "Baby, it's not your fault. We will get through this." But it was incredibly hard to see him suffer and be helpless to change anything. Sick or not, I loved him with all my heart.

Wrestling with God's choices for us was the most challenging internal fight of our lives. I had to learn to accept that God's "no" was the best decision for me, no matter what happened next. On my struggle days, I felt everything I knew about God was tested. I was seduced by darkness, depression, and disturbing thoughts. The pain of my experience was so deep it was numbing; nothing could reach it. Nothing I did could divert my attention.

As you'll soon see, I made it through to tell my story. But along the way, I learned that time and trouble can do a number on our faith. I also learned that our best gifts often come wrapped in those troubles and pains. As long as things are perfect or bearable, we can easily lean on ourselves for what we need. But when situations arise that are beyond us, and we find ourselves facing the impossible, we are reminded to pull on the only One who can pull us through: God. Once we come through, we rejoice at our gains, unwilling to trade our experiences for anything. Because we have borne our pain, we become stronger, wiser, more flexible, and more compassionate.

When we face these circumstances outside of our control, what's important is our attitude toward God. Our best is not always God's best, and we do not always agree with His decisions.

Sometimes there's an all-out brawl demanding to know why... only to hear God say something like, "My grace is sufficient."

What? we think angrily. *No, Lord, I need you to push "delete" on Heaven's keyboard! This isn't right; it can't be!* We don't understand; we think there must be another way, an easier way.

Yet even as we protest, God loves us. He does what is best even at the risk of our trust in Him. And love always does what is best and most beneficial.

Ultimately, there's a bigger plan, even if we can only see a small portion of that larger picture.

With such a limited viewpoint, who are we to judge God? Our existence is for a purpose, and getting us to fulfill that purpose is God's most significant task.

In your life right now, do you have a third wheel on your hands? Maybe you're in a toxic relationship or are struggling with debt. Possibly you have a child who is always in trouble, or you're going through a divorce or the death of a loved one. You could be dealing with the trauma of physical, sexual, or emotional abuse, or maybe you're facing chronic illness as a caretaker or a patient. Or maybe your third wheel is internal, coming in the form of fear, anxiety, low self-esteem, self-judgment, and other detrimental thoughts. How easily these things can overtake our lives! You see everyone else enjoying their days and wonder why you don't get the same chances. Instead, your circumstances dictate what happens daily, demanding your time, money, and energy. You simply want relief!

Regardless of your situation, there is only one way out, and that is faith in Jesus Christ.

There is something about faith that keeps reaching. It brings a fresh perspective to hopeless situations. It goes beyond human knowledge, deep into the spirit. It sees past the now into a blissful future. It allows us to take a break from our visual reality. It's the inner whisper that says, "Things are about to change. Rescue is near."

Faith reaches beyond our circumstances to God, who can create a way out of no way. Even if you have faced your pain for so long that agony, defeat, and surrender have become the norm, with faith, there is always hope. At one point, it seemed like my husband and I had a magnet on our backs that said, "Pain, come get us." The constant demands were draining everything we had, and as far as we could see, change was unattainable. But with an active God, faith in our prayers, and the right support system, we made it through every challenge... and went on to live our very best lives, even in the middle of the storm.

Yes, you heard me right: *You can live your best life in the worst of times* if you allow faith to transform your perspective. We all have the power to make our pain give us the best possible return in life just by shifting our outlook. No, we can't control every circumstance, but it's our outlook on the situation that adds sugar to the bitter tea. By trusting that there is a broader vision unfolding even in our most desperate, helpless moments, we discover we have more strength than we ever imagined. Our struggles define our purpose. As we endure difficult times and life assignments, we evolve. This process, though it can be painful, is priceless. It is not the good times that build our spiritual muscles but the difficult ones.

Delmar was frequently called "the miracle man" because of how many illnesses and physical disabilities he overcame, but it wasn't just his physical recovery that earned him his nickname. In facing his challenges, he was courageous, faithful, optimistic, and a strong believer.

He loved deeply, forgave quickly, and was committed to giving God worship and praise regardless of his circumstances. He encouraged many to overcome difficult obstacles, serving as a compass to those in trouble.

In life, most of us struggle with affliction at some point. But depending on your viewpoint, things look different. Are you the one in the bed of affliction? Or are you the loved one or caretaker, looking on from the other side? My heroic husband and I faced twenty-three years of ongoing illness. Despite our positive attitude, our journey was not easy. I was the caretaker for someone in despair and pain for many years. There were so many times when I just wanted to take his place so that he could have a break and a chance to live. But as the one afflicted, Delmar never wanted me to suffer (though eventually, I ended up facing my own illnesses, too).

If you are the caretaker responsible for a loved one who is afflicted, I want you to know that I see you. I understand exactly where you are, watching from the other side of the bed with your hands tied. I know the challenge of trying to appear strong even in your weakest moments, of facing that inner battle between faith and facts. You are being called upon to remain faith-filled, regardless of what comes, and that is no easy task. I know what it is to pour from an empty bucket feeling trapped, helpless, and pessimistic, all while physically trying to keep up the shell of being "alright."

Whether you're in the bed or next to it, I also want you to understand that it's not your fault. Challenges don't mean you did something wrong. Quite the opposite, in fact. It's pain that reveals our flaws, which are really just tender spots in need of healing. Flaws are perceived inadequacies irritated by self-sabotaging words and beliefs. If we buy into them, they can keep us from the fullness of God's grace and blessings. But in those darkest moments, God performs miracles we never fathomed. This story is proof, which is why I want to share it.

In the coming pages, I've revealed my innermost thoughts and secrets from my journey, including the ups and downs of our relationship, sex life, communication, and finances. I've also openly shared my emotional roller-coaster ride and the creative substitutions and coping mechanisms we tried along the way. Most of all, I've done my best to speak to the challenges of faith that come with going through difficult times... and how to trust that God's ultimate purpose for pain in our lives is deep, spiritual transformation.

Even with sickness as part of our lives, I do not regret one minute of our journey. Every moment was a gift, and our challenges drove us closer to each other, God, and our purpose. How did we do it, you ask? Love was the glue that held us together. God was the source of our strength. Faith was our hope. And the prayers and support of our family and friends were our generators.

Whether this book comes to you with a winning hand or a losing hand, I hope you find encouragement in these pages. God can carry you, just like He has carried me and so many others. No matter what challenges you are facing, your struggle can bring significant transformation if you allow it. Even if you think God has abandoned you, I promise He has not.

The journey is necessary for the reveal of greatness in your life. He is creating within you a new life, a chance for spiritual maturity beyond comprehension. There is a payoff to every pain you've endured.

BLISSFUL BEGINNINGS

Can you imagine marrying someone you met at nine years old? I was a little girl around that age. I was the typical kid playing with my baby dolls, wearing frilly dresses, and doing girly things. I am fortunate to be the daughter of two of the best pastors in the world, Dr. James F. and Sylvia H. Harris, of the historic *Redeemed Assembly of Jesus Christ, "where every seven days a miracle takes place."* It is a phenomenal church where the scriptures come alive with miracles, signs, and wonders. God started dealing with me at a young age. At eight, I was dreaming dreams that would later come to reality, and I was calling things out and seeing things that later manifested. I later learned that it was called prophecy and discernment.

One Sunday, a woman with a dry jerry curl bush and a guy with thick glasses dressed in a muddy brown suit, who looked about eighteen years old, caught my eye. As the service went on, I noticed this guy's high energy. He went from one end of the pew to the other throughout the entire service. He was amazed by the choir and the music, and he wasn't afraid to let everyone know. Later in talking with his mother, she revealed that he begged her to join the church during the first service. Eventually, they did join the church. He quickly made friends and jumped right in with both feet. After church, all youth would gather in the basement of the church to either talk or fight. We created our community in which everyone was accepting, and believing in Jesus was cool. Both the youth and their parents shared the same beliefs and were respectful of each other. The weird guy was quickly acclimated, just as if he had always been there. A rumor started to circulate that the new guy liked me. It was all strange to me. He looked way too old for me, mainly due to those thick glasses. If you are like me, you likely have a cookie-cutter guy you dream of marrying. Mine was extra tall and light-skinned with wavy or curly hair, and this guy didn't fit the dream in any way.

I asked, "How old are you?"

And he replied, "Twelve."

I said to myself, *My God, and you have hair on your face?*

The rumors kept circulating so I approached him and asked him if it was true.

He replied, "Yes!"

At that age, I wondered what I was supposed to do with that information. Soon after we called ourselves "boyfriend and girlfriend," which included exchanging love letters each service (nothing hot or steamy). All of mine started with "Dear Delmonte." It was not until later that I discovered his name to be Delmar. We discussed everything through our letters. Then we advanced to phone conversations as we grew older. He had to sneak to call me, and when his mother would ask who he was speaking to, he would reply, "Stanley, Ron, Carlos, or Billy," who were his closest friends. Unbeknownst to her, we spent hours on the phone.

Delmar delved into ministry. He began to direct the choir, and at the age of fifteen, he had his choir, called the *Disciples for Christ.* We sang all over the city. He then became the director of the National Youth Choir. I became Delmar's assistant to speed things up during rehearsal. I would teach parts and Delmar would select the music, manage the musicians and choir members, and direct during rehearsal and performances. At the time, I was a first soprano. We had the city's best soprano section and were sometimes asked to sing with other groups and choirs.

Our love grew for each other as I evolved into a young lady. I couldn't get enough of him. He was always on my mind. I was also in charge of the church store, and I can remember closing one Sunday when Delmar stepped up to me and kissed me. I kissed him back. I had no idea what I was doing. I just did what he did. Unknowing, one of the missionaries saw us and told my parents.

Then, one day, while in the store, we looked up and saw both of my parents. My father then asked, "Have you all been kissing?"

I was so embarrassed, and I felt like I was about to faint.

Delmar replied, "Yes, Sir."

My father said, "You don't want to start something you can't control. In other words, don't start the motor before you're ready to drive the car."

My mom just said, "We will talk when we get home."

In my mind, I thought, *No, Ma'am!* With my body developing, it became hard not to touch or kiss him. I'd forgotten about my dolls. Kissing was my new toy.

Fast forward a few years. We could finally drive. Once he started driving, he was always at my house. One day he came to visit me and told my mother that he couldn't see. All he could see were shadows. In her nurturing way, my mother said, "Look, take this money and immediately go to the eye doctor."

My sister's boyfriend, Atron (Chuck), followed him to the eye doctor for his safety. To our alarm, we received a call saying that the ambulance had rushed Delmar to the hospital because of blood behind his eyes and his blood pressure was extremely high. His diastolic and systolic pressure were both over 200. I can remember coming home from school; upon entering the house, my mom told me Delmar was in the hospital.

I immediately ran to my room and just cried. My mother decided to let my sister and me go to visit him. I'll admit I was shocked, but I was so anxious to get there. As we opened the door to his room, all of his machines went off. Beep, beep, beep! My sister Tione and I looked at each other in complete shock, thinking we'd somehow killed him! But Delmar had the biggest smile on his face.

The nurse kicked us out of the room because Delmar got too excited when he saw us. Yeah, I had that effect on him. Although we had to leave, seeing him brought relief.

Then in his senior year of high school, his leg started to swell for no apparent reason. It was huge, and he expressed how badly it hurt. He functioned as normally as he could until he could no longer ignore the pain. He soon discovered that his kidneys were failing. Soon after, he was discharged and diagnosed with celeritous, which was caused by FSGS, a kidney disease—meaning his kidneys were too small. His kidneys took a hard hit from his high blood pressure. Immediately, a group of loving people from our church went to be tested to see if they were matches for him.; a kind act of love. The diagnosis was a serious blow, but he was confident that he would not end up on dialysis, quoting Hebrews 10:35-36 (NLT), which states, "So do not throw away this confident trust in the Lord. Remember the great reward it brings you! 36. Patient endurance is what you need now, so that you will continue to do God's will. Then you will receive all that he has promised." The shock of possibly being on dialysis was inconceivable.

Upon graduating, his kidneys took another plunge. His worst nightmare became his reality as he was placed on peritoneal dialysis. This type of treatment includes a six-foot tube embedded in the stomach. Part of it protruded out of the stomach, which connects to portable dialysis bags. One drains out, and a fresh bag of fluid flows in. This process would also include hooking up to bags at nighttime while he slept to purify his system. Wherever he went, he would take a hanger or whatever he could find, continue his dialysis, and get on with his daily schedule. This type of treatment allowed him to live a somewhat normal life, as everything was portable. He was disappointed, but he always had a strong coping mechanism, which was good in this instance. He was afraid of the severity, and limitations, and didn't know how it would impact his life. He learned to cope with the low energy levels, the long hours for iron drips, and the new dialysis schedule while still trusting God for his healing. He was always able to see the positive in adverse situations. He still felt blessed because he could do dialysis at home every four hours, work, and still travel.

Fast forward to the eve of my seventeenth birthday, Valentine's Day, which was significant because I could now date. My mom reiterated the rules and reminded me of how to conduct myself as a young lady. It was a beautiful day. Of course, the history buff had to take me to an educational spot, the museum, where he shared all of his knowledge with me. We then drove around the city and ended up eating at Daryl's, a pretty upscale restaurant for a couple of teenagers. It was an amazing evening. I stared into his beautiful brown eyes and just enjoyed having a good conversation and flirting. Could life get any better? After dinner, walking to the car, Delmar started vomiting uncontrollably. It seemed like an eternity before it ended. After seeing him experience this, I knew he was seriously ill. I just sat in the car and cried, watching how sick he was. For the next few years, Delmar frequently went to the hospital because of high blood pressure, deficient energy levels (low iron), and peritonitis (an abdomen infection from this type of dialysis).

OUR PERSONAL GOD

Married and penniless just doesn't work well, wouldn't you say? My dad often says the first fight will always be about money. "No money, no honey."

Delmar said, "Don't worry about money; I will take care of you."

The hustler in me said, "Prove it first." In my mind, I was thinking, "I thought they were supposed to ask you to marry, in some crazy romantic way." *Not!* Delmar was a man of faith. His faith was evident when he called me to tell me that we would get married on the second Saturday in October all while he and his mom were being evicted out of their apartment.

I said, "Ummm, you are in no position to marry me."

He proceeded to tell me that the youth are in charge of that Sunday service so we can get away that week. Oh, I failed to mention, that everything revolved around youth Sunday in our planning because the choir didn't have to sing. Understand, Delmar always told me during our relationship that I would be his wife. So, I told my parents. My dad replied, "You better go and find a dress now. You are full-figured, and it may take a while for your dress to come in."

Umm, ok, Dad?

The next day my mom and I hit the streets to find a dress. I was wondering if this was really happening! Delmar was in such dire financial shape. To purchase my ring, my mom had to cosign for him. He was the only person in her lifetime she ever cosigned for. Let's make a point right here. Ladies, your man may not be ideal, but if love is worth it, then go for it. There is nothing like success built between two people.

Many people are single now and have missed out on love because they were picky, waiting for their ideal man. They are still single, sitting in a rocking chair talking about how Boaz is coming. Boaz has come and gone. In case you're wondering who Boaz was, read the book of Ruth in the Old Testament of the Bible. He may not have a pocket filled with money, the perfect job, or the ideal height, but he will be your best life partner. If it's only cosmetic then prepare for disappointment. *Neither of us was without flaws, but we were perfect for each other.* And by all means, make sure you can offer what you expect to receive. The biggest lie told is that two halves make a whole.

½ x ½ =1/4, but 1x1=1.

In other words, you can't become a whole until there are two whole parts, not pieces. Again, are you healed or expecting someone to make you whole? That's too much for any person to do. Do your work! Don't just fall in love with the wedding day, but prepare for a lifetime of happiness whatever that looks like.

I will never forget the real proposal. It was a Wednesday night after Bible Study, and Delmar asked to say something on the stage microphone. He said some beautiful things about me and then proposed from the stage! Now, I was quiet, shy, and an extreme introvert. I didn't walk to the front, but Delmar came to my pew to slip the ring on my finger. I said, "I think this is happening." We hustled to get the funds to marry because we wanted to be together badly. We needed to be married. I worked at the salon from sun up till sun down and Delmar worked two jobs. My parents, sister Denise, and friends helped us with the remaining balance.

We were married on Saturday, October 11, 1997, at 5:00 p.m. The weather was a perfect 70 degrees, and the morning was filled with activities including nails, breakfast, and a little shopping. I couldn't have asked for a better day. I was on cloud nine to marry the man who made me feel like a queen. The church was full, with over 500 family members and friends in attendance. It was bittersweet because I had to leave my family, but I was marrying the man I had an overwhelming love for who had stolen my heart. I was so proud to become his wife, and he was so pleased to become my husband. We had a bet going as to who would cry first. I lost the bet.

On our wedding day, adorning the aisles were beautiful flowers and candles. I was wearing a stunning off-the-shoulder, white A-line dress with plenty of delicate trimmings and a custom-made sparkling headpiece. The song that Meredith Robinson sang was "I Believe in You and Me" by Whitney Houston. Even though I had some hiccups such as losing my dress for over an hour, my cake not being fully cooked, and the limousine not being ordered, it was still a picture-perfect day. (Thankfully, my sister Denise whipped out her credit card on the way to the church and paid for a limousine on the spot!) I still couldn't stop thinking about leaving my parents, no longer their little girl, during my perfect day. I was now an independent woman, taking a husband.

Everything else was a blur with all the craziness happening until it was all over. It was time to leave, so we got in the limousine, held hands, and kissed. My heart was racing with excitement! It was official; I was now Mrs. Branch and never had to leave him again. We were going home together. We later arrived at my parents' house to pick up my suitcase. The way my clothes were when I came home told the story of what happened in the back of that limo. My family noticed as soon as we entered the front door. They had plenty of jokes. My face flushed, and I was embarrassed, but not Delmar. He was like, "Yeah, that's mine now!"

We were heading back to our new apartment where Delmar was staying, but my mom was adamant that we go to a hotel, so we agreed. To enjoy ourselves, we needed money. Therefore, we opened our wedding envelopes to calculate the cash received. The people were generous!

After leaving my parents' house we arrived at the hotel. I showered while Delmar did his dialysis. I was scared to death to come out in the skimpy white lace ensemble, which revealed my ample cleavage. I finally got up the nerve to open the door and just stood there. The limo experience in the dark was less pressure than what was about to happen in the light. I came out of the bathroom, and there he stood with the biggest smile. "Baby, you look beautiful." And he just stared at me with pride. He said, "Let me hurry up and finish my dialysis!" He then came out of the bathroom.

Lord, I was lost and very nervous. It wasn't the best feeling, but everything was perfect after the sex cuddle as there were no barriers between us. Listening to his heartbeat with my face on his soft skin and smelling his sexy cologne was heavenly. We were together forever. One of our wedding gifts from my parents was a honeymoon trip to a destination of our choice. We chose Williamsburg because it was close, and we still had to decorate and unpack the apartment. We arrived in Williamsburg, and by then, I was a little more comfortable. He made me feel flawless and was so patient with me, I'm sure he was thinking, *Lord, I married a freak!* We were so strapped for money that we returned to our apartment in the middle of our honeymoon to take back gifts for cash. We had enough crystal to open a small storefront. We were rich again!

Too soon, the honeymoon was over and real life began. It was now time for me to put into practice everything I witnessed my mom, Sylvia H. Harris, do. She was the mark for all wives and mothers. I wanted my home to feel as safe and loving as the home I grew up in. The first night we were back, I decided to cook a delicious meal consisting of slow-baked barbeque ribs, mac and cheese, green beans, chocolate walnut cake, and a fresh pitcher of Kool-Aid. I slipped on some lingerie and was ready for my husband. I was determined to make him the happiest man on Earth. The apartment was so fresh and clean. When he opened the door after returning from work, I greeted him with a hug and a passionate kiss. I was ready to knock him down, but he was anxious to eat. I fixed him a plate, and he proceeded to go into the bedroom to watch wrestling. I was like, "Oh, No! You didn't read your script." I walked into the room and picked up our thirty-two-inch, big-back TV like I was the infamous wrestler, The Undertaker. I said, "You want a wrestler? The wrestler is right here!" He threw the remote across the room, we exchanged some heated words, and I went to the second bedroom.

I think I slept in the second bedroom more than my bed in the first year of our marriage, but it always ended the same way. Delmar could not stay mad. Sometime in the middle of the night, I would feel his warm body beside me. He was my Pooh Bear. Things were all right again. An argument here and there is the perfect formula for good sex and conversation.

We were figuring it out. It is true that you don't know a person until you have lived with them. After knowing him for most of my life, I thought that I knew everything. Not! Our two worlds collided many times. Grocery shopping was nearly impossible because we both wanted our mothers' brands. Not willing to give in on a few things, we bought double. Eventually, we learned to compromise.

The next day, while showering in our guest bathroom, which had no windows, everything went black. I said, "Oh my, what is going on?" I went through the apartment, flipping switches, and nothing worked. I went to the power box, flipping the switches on and off, but still nothing. I called Delmar, and he said, "I will take care of it."

Come to find out he forgot to pay the electric bill. It was easy to call my dad, but I said, "No. I've known the God of my parents, and now it's time for me to know Him for myself." So, instead of reaching out to my dad for comfort, I said, "Lord, fix it." The lights came back on almost immediately!

Our next challenge was the car. It was snowing uncontrollably with blizzard-like conditions. The wipers and heat didn't work in the white Buick with the burgundy interior and a boom box in the back seat. The only way Delmar could get home was to hang his head out of the window to see. He was freezing by the time he arrived home. Our transportation dilemma did not dampen our love for each other or our happiness. We both worked two jobs and kept it moving. There were days I knew he didn't feel well, yet he never missed time from work. He was determined to work and make his money. I remember one time we didn't know how we would pay the rent. Delmar was adamant about working and providing. Sure, he could have qualified for disability as a dialysis patient, which would have covered all his medical bills. Still, he wanted to provide and feel the responsibility of being a man. He refused to use his illness as an excuse; rather he kept planning for the future he expected. As for me, I was rather determined to find a way. We wanted to live a proactive rather than reactive lifestyle. I returned some clothes I purchased on sale and much to my surprise, they gave me back the full price for sale items, and I took it! Excited and appreciative were we. God always provided. We were never late paying our rent with all our struggles. God is faithful.

He kept providing for us. We were even able to attend the annual family vacations. Before arrival, we would have all his dialysis boxes shipped to the vacation spot. I can remember going to Florida with friends and family. As a dialysis patient, he was told not to get in the swimming pool because of the opening port in his abdomen which could cause severe illness. But not Delmar. With tears in his eyes, he looked at my mom one day while everyone was swimming and said, "Momma, I want to get in the pool." Feeling sorry for him, my mother came up with the idea to wrap his abdomen in saran wrap. She tested it to be sure no liquid could get through so he could enjoy the private pool in the back of the vacation home. He loved it! His new freedom was a problem for us because he never wanted to get out of the water, but he always made the best of devastating circumstances.

THE TURNING POINT

The covenant words "in sickness and in health" were tested on every level. I knew about dialysis when I married Delmar, but what was to come was a real curveball. Delmar struggled to get out of bed because his energy levels were so low. The doctor told him that he would have to start administering Epogen shots at home to build up his deficient energy levels.

Well, at home meant I had to do it. I am that patient who almost faints when the doctor pricks my finger, so I knew this was a recipe for disaster. Now, you want me to inject my husband with a needle? Jesus, help me be a nurse! It took me so long to get up the nerve to do it; he said, "Give me the needle, and I'll stick myself." Between the day-long iron drips and Epogen shots, his energy slowly returned. Then, he developed an infection in his abdomen. Oh, there was always something going on. By being on peritoneal dialysis, he often had peritonitis, an infection of the abdomen. This condition was excruciating and caused severe cramping in his stomach. Most days, he could only lay in a balled-up knot on the floor. When it got too bad, we would go to the emergency room. It was nothing for me to come home from the salon sometimes at 1 and 2 a.m. to find him lying on the floor balled up in a knot paralyzed with pain. When asked how long he had been there, he could never recall, which only meant we were in for an overnight stay in the emergency room. Finding him in this condition occurred frequently.

I would sit in the emergency area on pins and needles. All I wanted to know was whether Delmar was out of pain. It hurt me to see him in that state, but I could do nothing. After many tests, the doctors discovered spidery veins around his colon and an infection in his peritoneal cavity. After repeated abdominal surgeries and a month's stay, they released him. Two weeks later, he was back in the hospital for previous diagnoses, adding pneumonia and a collapsed lung. Once again, he was sent home with me as his nurse. I could hear him praying for relief as the pain was so great. His weight dropped drastically. His body was frail; his bones protruding, and his eyes always looked dilated. He honestly looked like death but still had his winning smile. His spirit was still expectant that God would come through for him. People would pull me aside wherever we went and ask how he was doing. They were so concerned. Whenever his friends visited him, they would address him like it was their last visit. Delmar would reassure them by telling them what God would do for him. They looked at him like, "Have you seen yourself lately?" He's frail, and I'm bulking up from surviving from vending machines. Together, we looked like the number ten.

About a month later, we returned to the hospital. This time, they placed tubes in Delmar's peritoneal cavity to drain the infected pockets caused by the scar tissue from all the previous abdominal surgeries. The pain was so great that he would continuously vomit when he ate food until all that was left was his stomach lining's green bile. The doctors still didn't know the infection source causing his elevated temperatures. So, they sent him home with a PICC line, which led from his arm straight to his heart, with drainage tubes hung from his abdomen. It seemed as if he was at the hospital every day taking tests, getting probed, getting x-rays, CAT scans, and MRIs. Between IVs and needles, his veins collapsed. Because of the abdominal trauma, they started to discuss taking him off peritoneal dialysis and placing him on hemodialysis dialysis. The change in treatment for us meant the loss of freedom because he would be tied to a machine for hours at a time.

After eleven years of dialysis, hospital stays, Epogen shots, blood transfusions, iron drips, abdominal infections, CT scans, X-rays, and MRIs, he ended up in the hospital incredibly sick. Delmar was so ill. He continued to have more abdominal surgeries and still no relief. He then developed hiccups that would not stop. Day in and day out, he would hiccup. After a long time, they found some meds to fix that. Life continued to happen. Bills were still coming in, but we were making it. God kept providing. Nothing was more important than his health, therefore we continued to battle what we saw and knew and praised and trusted God for his healing. He was our only hope for healing. We were each other's cheerleaders. I had to be strong and be an advocate for Delmar. Being an advocate included researching, asking questions, getting advice from doctors and pharmacists, finding the next steps, and ensuring that the nurses and doctors adequately cared for Delmar. It was exhausting. So many days, I felt like I needed a doctor. Sleeping in hospital chairs day in and day out had taken a toll.

THE DEATH OF FREEDOM

Freedom is better than confinement any day. Peritoneal dialysis was like a type of house arrest. We still had freedom even though he had to break every four hours for dialysis and then connect at night so that his machine would dialyze him overnight. Delmar's health continued to decline rapidly. What we feared the most was now knocking on the door: hemodialysis. In this type of dialysis, they drain all the blood out of the body, purify it through a machine, and run it back into the body: a four-hour event that takes place at least three days a week. The day of his first treatment was one of the saddest days of my life as I realized that our lives now revolved around a schedule void of freedom. My energetic, fun-loving, hardworking husband was confined and at the mercy of a machine that had a lifespan, and his life would be void of spontaneity and some privileges. As I waited for him to dialyze, I couldn't stop crying and sobbing. I was no good for him.

We always praised God as we walked through the hemodialysis section to visit the peritoneal section in the back of the building. As we walked through, we would always pray that God would bless and heal those in that section, while we thanked God for not being restricted to the machine. I was disappointed and devastated. Hadn't he been through enough? "God help us," I cried. The nurse called his name. Almost at the door, he looked back at me and followed the nurse to get weighed. *Sickness was now the bride of the relationship.* I could tell depression was knocking on the door of Delmar's heart as he saw his future in every patient there. The patients filling the room looked gray and feeble. Some were even missing limbs. Was this our future? He had already witnessed the ambulances picking up those who had perished during their treatment, and we were wondering if he was next. While I was in the sitting area, face swollen from crying and devastated, I heard the machines go off, and then I heard his name. Delmar had gone into violent convulsions; his heart was racing along with several other events. His life was on the line. They rushed him to the emergency room, yet again, only to find that he was allergic to the antibiotic administered by the hospital as a last resort to cure his infection.

What do you do when you can't do anything to help your loved one? In a conversation with my father, he stated something that shed light and gave breath to my situation. He said, "Danielle, in most cases, we praise our problem and speak to God when God commands us to speak to the problem and praise God. Whatever we praise gets bigger." Whatever we meditate on becomes fortified until it becomes something that controls us. Jesus always used His words to create what He wanted to see. He told us to speak to the mountain, not praise the mountain. So reserve your strength for praise. Give Him credit for doing what He said He would do. Praise God and speak to that problem. Cry, but believe. Pray and believe. Keep speaking until you can convince your heart of what you are saying. Keep hoping even though the prayer request seems light years away, and it looks like the answer is closer to death than life. For us, the hospital became our home. I still had to work, so my family would sit with him during the day to ensure he was adequately cared for while I worked. My schedule was as follows: work, home to shower, then back to the hospital. My dinner and breakfast came from the vending machines unless someone brought me a meal, but none of that mattered if Delmar was good. I had no time to feel sorry for myself. The doctors had threatened him with death at least three times, and all we had was our hope in God. Trusting God was comforting yet scary as His ability and wisdom were beyond us, beyond our situations, beyond our control, and the doctor's examination. We were able to put all our cares on Him and take a break. I know all too well the meaning of Psalm 55:22 (MSG), which states, "Pile your troubles on GOD's shoulders—he'll carry your load; he'll help you out. He'll never let good people topple into ruin." I had to know about my role and His role. I was limited, and He had unlimited power, knowledge, and ability to bring us out of this overwhelming situation. I didn't qualify for the position of God. His resume was too extensive.

At this point, Delmar's weight had gone from 220 to 130 pounds. He was simply skin and bones, gray and feeble. He looked just like the others at the center. When I saw depression trying to take his last bit of energy, I would just grab his hand and remind him what God said. Isaiah 53:5 KJV says, "...with His stripes we are healed." Healing was completed before Delmar ever became sick. We would rehearse every promise we could remember, sometimes with tears in our eyes and doubt in our hearts, but we continued to pray and sometimes sing. What do you do when you're doing what's right but looking at the wrong results? Maybe you're a tither, but the tithes are all you have. Maybe you are an intercessor, but everything in your life seems to be going to hell. Maybe you are always the one giving, but no one is there to rescue you when in need. Maybe the very call on your life is causing you grief. These are the times when your pain is an assignment. With the physical eye you look like you're losing, but spiritually, you are soaring. God is working a bigger purpose in your life that only pain can produce. Without the pain, we would take His position. The goal is wholeness and complete dependence on God. It is when people fail us and we are at the end of our hope and resources that we pull on our Savior. Say with me, "And yet I win!" Scream it right where you are, louder than the voice that's trying to convince you that your situation will never change and that things will always be the way they are. Fortify your faith with scriptures. The only way you win is by using the weapons of God: prayer, praise, and obedience. If the devil only knew what the pain was producing, he would reverse his course. Pain seeks to do two things: stop you or put you in reverse. Sometimes, we feel we are too far in to go back but lack the strength to push forward. I encourage you to take another look at your circumstances, see past the physical, and forge forward.

Delmar continued to decline. At one point, all he wanted was his morphine. Yes, to keep him comfortable, his doctor prescribed morphine and Percocet. We all hate when the doctors say, "Let's just keep them comfortable." It's like seeing the white flag admitting that whatever the culprit is has won. Delmar had a nasogastric (NG) tube in his nose to remove the bowel from his stomach, a feeding tube in his neck, and tubes hanging from his sides. He continued having extreme abdominal pain and receiving hemodialysis. This became his new norm.

It was now a year since we had been home or had sex, a year since anything had been as it had been, and still no answers. Being very affectionate, Delmar made it hard not to long for his touch; what I wouldn't have done to just lay in his arms and take a nap. I needed something to distract me from all the stress. Some days, I just wanted to pretend. Let's act like you are well so we can make love. Sex became a stress reliever at times in our relationship. Yes, there were days when we made love, but then there were those days when we just needed a quick fix to counter the stress of life. Some people need a reason to have sex, but we had stress sex before he became ill. I know you are asking, "Danielle, what is that?" That's when you come home and take your clothes off, no foreplay, get it up, take it off, and just bang the stress away and then fall asleep. Sometimes, you need something to escape all the drama, if only for a few minutes. One of those times he came home, he was so feeble, but I needed affection and intimacy. After over a year of being under constant stress and not being intimate in any way, watching the worst happen, I just needed a distraction from all the pressure. I said, "Now, how am I going to initiate sex without being insensitive?" Well, I knew his hot spots. I told him just to lay there, in my humble nurse voice.

When the time came, I made sure we were both happy! I know, terrible, right? Lying in the bed beside my love was a prayer answered. Delmar was delayed in responding after being home for a few days when I called his name. Being Nurse Dani B, I went into research mode and found that the meds they gave him for his constant hiccups were causing a delayed response. Once I took him off, he was back to normal. Our conversations were all we had. After this incident, I investigated all his meds and asked the doctor questions. I've learned that you must be versed and knowledgeable about your health, especially when seeing multiple specialists, and communicate, communicate, communicate.

The ordeal was not over. After weeks of tests, they discovered that pockets were still in his abdomen, so they continued to run tests. They had already administered the most potent antibiotics, which failed. Delmar's health was baffling to the doctors and nurses. He was readmitted to the hospital about a month later, still suffering from severe stomach pain, high blood pressure, and a spiking temperature. We knew a high temperature was dangerous because it was a sign of infection. That day, they continued to test him, looking for answers. We were released again without any real answers.

One night, we checked into the hospital because his top and bottom blood pressure numbers were over 200. They rushed him back immediately and admitted him. Whenever I could, I slept in a chair in the hospital beside him, even when he had to share a room. I would help both patients. I knew if I went home, I would only sit up and wonder how he was doing or if he needed anything. I just had to be there even if I couldn't help. I didn't ever want him to think he was alone in the fight of his life. My regimen was to scrub and disinfect everything in the room, adorn the chair with sheets and blankets to make it feel as close to a bed as possible, and talk the night away.

The next morning, Delmar stated, "Let me get myself together before they come and get me." As he sat up in the bed, he screamed. I immediately ran out of the room for help. When I came back into the room with nurses and doctors, he'd passed out. They then rushed him out of the room. A few hours later, he returned paralyzed on his left side. I could not believe my eyes. Paralyzed?! *Has heaven shut down for the day?* Immediately, a barrage of thoughts flooded my mind. I thought about the effect paralysis would have on Delmar's esteem and how it would affect his quality of life, and then I thought of how it would impact my life.

After thirty minutes of a therapist working with him, his side returned to full strength. He sat up in the bed, tightly gripped me around my waist, and began to talk randomly about events that were unknown to me. I remember him specifically asking me to go across the street to get the snowball icees we used to eat. I was dumbfounded, but I'm known for forgetting things. So, I pretended to know, to avoid upsetting him. I just held him, and he embraced me in return, and then he announced, "I'm going out!" Delmar passed out again and they rushed him out of the room. I lost it! I sobbed uncontrollably. There are times when you can keep it together, and then there is that one event that breaks the dam of tears and emotions. My mom was there and called my dad. Just as he asked if Delmar had had a stroke, the nurse walked in and said he had. By then, his mom had arrived; we were both devastated. The next time I saw him was in the ICU. He didn't even recognize me. The only person he recognized was my mother. I was shattered! He had completely lost his mind. He held her hand, pretending it was a remote control, and a picture hanging on the wall was the TV. He reverted to childhood memories and began to talk about a little boy we hadn't seen in decades. My mom played along as they strapped him to the bed and prepped him for dialysis. They asked me to sign a stack of papers. I was so distraught I waived all my rights to my mother.

The thought of him losing his mind was overwhelming. You see, Delmar was a knowledgeable man, and our conversations meant everything to me as they were intellectually stimulating to me. I had grown accustomed to his vast knowledge of just about any subject from music and history, current events, to directions and the Bible. He was intellectually sexy. I knew how to physically care for him, but this new mental challenge could take my last ounce of strength. *Oh, my God, what are you doing up there? Now is not the time for silence. I need you to use your words, God, and I need to see the plans.*

The hospital staff made me leave my husband. My mom begged them not to strap him down, but they said it was a safety precaution. I had to leave my man with strangers, which was concerning because he could not communicate, and he was not in his right mind. In the state I was in, my mom thought it best that I go home and take a sedative to calm down. After dropping me off at my house, I hopped in the shower and just cried. I was a wreck. Did this mean that I would never have a heart-to-heart conversation with him again? Was this our forever? What is our life going to be like going forward? I was so afraid of what would happen to him: his future and our future. What would love look like going forward? I slipped my clothes on and headed directly back to the hospital. When I saw him again, he was in a coma. I didn't know what to think. For the first time, I felt like my health was in jeopardy. My insides were shaking. I was exhausted, mentally and physically, and completely helpless. For the next two days, he remained in a coma. The next day my sister and mom met me at the hospital. Delmar was still in a coma, but the nurses said he could hear us. Why did they say that? Tione started singing some of his favorite songs as loud as she could. An all-out concert! I knew it was driving my mom crazy. Being a discreet woman, my mom couldn't take it any longer and said, "That's enough!" and we laughed.

A few hours later, I got a call from the hospital.

I will never forget it. I was staying with my sister Tione and her husband Chucky because no one wanted me to stay alone. The phone rang, and the neural surgeon bluntly said, "Mrs. Branch, your husband has fluid on his brain, and we need to perform a ventricular ostomy (brain surgery) to release the pressure." The doctor explained the severity of the surgery as it involved drilling a hole and placing a tube in his head to drain the fluid due to swelling. If he didn't have the operation, he would die or live the rest of his life as a vegetable. The doctor also stated that it could be months before he would regain consciousness. Overwhelmed, I immediately called my parents and asked what I should do.

With this latest update, I broke down again. I didn't know whether I was going or coming. I gave the doctors the go-ahead after discussing it with my family, who then rushed down to the hospital, along with a few close friends. I rode with Tione and Chuck to the hospital. Chuck sang those ancient praise and worship songs the entire commute. You would have thought he was on a stage getting paid to usher the people into the presence of God! It lightened the atmosphere, but in retrospect, it was hilarious at the same time. It took our minds off the situation for a few minutes. We arrived at the hospital, and one of our friends started to cry. My dad was righteously mad. He said in a stern voice, "Either you are going to believe, or you are going to go home." It was as if he had on war gear and was ready to fight for Delmar's healing. We all got the message and adjusted our attitudes accordingly. That night, we began praying for Delmar and the other intensive care unit (ICU) patients. There is one thing my family does well: pray! It is effective and always brings results.

We prayed heaven down while he was in surgery, filling the room with praise for what we expected God to do. We created a pathway for victory. When there is no physical help, and you can't see a way, go ahead and praise God for a successful ending. Give Him credit for what you are praying and waiting on. It will make a path right down the middle of your problem and let you walk through to claim the prize. I feel the presence of Jesus just sharing that truth.

So many times during our marriage, I didn't have the money, the smarts, the connections, the answers, or the solution. All I had was expectancy. Expectancy is the excitement and assurance that happens when you know God will come through. Whatever you do when you're going through challenges, believe God. He may not come when you think He should, but He's coming. He's famous for working miracles. He likes grand entrances. When the chips are down, and they are about to count you out, here He comes. He has no rival. He wins in big ways. Let God out of the boundaries of your past experiences and your personal limitations. Let Him be God without restrictions.

At that time, we felt if we could get into the sanctuary of the church, we could gain some strength. Our Holy Convocation, a gathering of saints who come together for a worship experience, convened at the church while we were still going through a lot at the hospital. We missed the feeling and strength of being in the great congregation of believers. All we knew was church. So Delmar did the bold ask: "Doc, can you just let me out for a few hours so I can go to church?" The doctor looked puzzled, but he felt sorry for him. He said, "I don't advise you to leave, but if I don't know..." We got the hint. We conspired to sneak out and sneak back into the hospital. I rushed home and picked up his suit and the necessary belongings. We pretended to go for an afternoon stroll around the hospital. I drove the car up to the nearest exit, and we were off.

We snuck into the back of the auditorium, and Delmar switched out of his gown into his church attire. Then it was my turn. Delmar had someone grab him a stool, and he led worship that evening. He entered the stage, gave God his all, and ushered the people into the presence of the Lord. Although his body was frail, Delmar's spirit was rejuvenated as he led the congregation in worship, giving praise to his loving God. As soon as he stopped, we slipped to the back of the auditorium, changed our clothes, hopped into the car, and entered the hospital as if we had been catching some air. That was a great night! We were able to take a break from the pain …in praise. We had a chance to see our problem through the eyes of a great big God.

Praise is faith on display, and it reminds us of Who is in control. What ailment can argue with His healing? Who can provide as He does? Psalm 24:1 (MSG) states, "GOD claims Earth and everything in it, God claims World and all who live on it." Who can take care of all your needs? Philippians 4:19 (MSG) states, "You can be sure that God will take care of everything you need, his generosity exceeding even yours in the glory that pours from Jesus." Psalm 23:1 (MSG) states, "GOD, my shepherd! I don't need a thing." What can argue with His peace? Who can open and close doors? Only Jesus. He is Yahweh, the God that causes things to be, meaning you don't have to see it. He doesn't need a substance to create anything, for He is substance. He shows up as what you need. He is the source of all resources. He made everything you see. Who can move on a person's heart to take care of your needs? Only God. He has no opponent. He has no rival. He's in a class all by Himself. Whatever you are going through is wrapped in a victory sentence. We start in victory even when it looks like defeat. God knows us and tailors our trials and troubles to us individually. He weighs out our troubles and blessings. He always carries the heaviest end of the problem. Your path to victory was made before the trouble. Don't get in the driver's seat. Waive all your rights to Him. Try to enjoy the ride as much as possible. Bridge the gap between your last miracle and your next miracle by remembering how He brought you out of your previous impossible situation. Give Him advance praise and journal your blessings in the process.

God cannot fail. When it looks like failure, it's still a victory. If you are sick, thank Him for the measure of health you still have. If you are broke, thank Him for your ability to seek employment. You have the privilege to ask God to be what you need. Complaining closes the eyes to the blessings at hand. Complaining closes the mind to possibilities and hope, but praise changes our perspective. Your problem, mixed with praise, is called a miracle. When you praise, expect the unexpected. I love the way Ephesians 3:20 AMPC puts it: "Now to Him Who, by (in consequence of) the [action of His] power that is at work within us, is able to [carry out His purpose and] do superabundantly, far over *and* above all that we [dare] ask or think [infinitely beyond our highest prayers, desires, thoughts, hopes, or dreams]." Expect the exceeding abundance of His grace. For whatever you are going through, His grace is sufficient. You have all you need to win. Every high place, those things that seem out of control, overwhelming, out of reach, over you, God is bringing them down. His life is the guarantee. Let the words of this song touch you; "I Will Make the Darkness Light Before Thee," by Charles Price Jones:

I will make the darkness light before thee,
What is wrong I'll make it right before thee,
All thy battles I will fight before thee,
And the high place I'll bring down.

With an everlasting love I'll love thee,
Though with trials deep and sore I'll prove thee,
But there's nothing that can hurt or move thee,
And the high place I'll bring down.

Although Satan in his rage would tear thee,
And with all his winning arts would snare thee,
Even down to thine old age I'll bear thee,
And the high place I'll bring down.

I will make the darkness light before thee,
I will make the crooked straight before thee,
I will spread My wings protecting o'er thee,
And the high place, I'll bring down.

When thou walkest by the way I'll lead thee,
On the fatness of the land I'll feed thee,
And a mansion in the sky I'll deed thee,
And the high place I'll bring down.

OK, back to the story. Miraculous things happened! When the doctor came in to ask for the family of Delmar Branch, the whole room replied, "Yes!" The doctor said he had never seen such a large crowd for one person. Not only did Delmar pull through, but that weekend, everyone in that unit was healed and moved out of the ICU unit. The Lord did it again! Looking back, I can't help but think, "Did God have Delmar there for us to pray for a family that didn't have a connection with Him?" God is strategic in His moves. One of His moves answers many prayers.

One move can give one a "yes," one a "no," and one a "not now." His knowledge is far beyond our tiny minds. We understand as we go, but God had a plan before we were even born. He's already planned our future. We live in His past tense. Who can keep up with God? He is God.

Your situation is serving you and others at the same time, as well as multiple purposes. Your coming out will give someone else hope that's about to go into a painful situation. It's not optional; you must make it! The survival of others is dependent on your victory. Don't waste your go through.

When we finished, Delmar had pulled through brain surgery. Remember the doctor said it may be a matter of months before he woke up? Well, the next morning, around 8:00 a.m., I got a call from Delmar's mother saying he had asked for me by name. I said,

"Who for who?" I couldn't believe it! I rushed back to the hospital; he remembered me! With a hole drilled in his head and a drainage tube, he said, "Hey, Poodie!" I just wanted to cry, scream praises to God, and hold him. God had brought him through yet another time. Note: What's impossible with man is always possible with God. Luke 18:27 states, "He replied, "What is impossible for people is possible with God." God has the final say in any diagnosis when you live by faith.

Because of the excess fluid, I noticed the elevation of Delmar's head and the tube that went from his head to the machine for drainage. He was alert, talking, and could recognize everyone. However, he was a little different. He was still hallucinating a bit from the fluid that remained in his head and making jokes that made no sense. Each time he fell asleep, I would have to repeat everything I said. I had to ask a series of questions: what year was it, who was the president, when was his birthday, his name, my name, and so on. Each time he woke up, he would begin talking about monkeys. Monkeys in the window, in the church basement, in the unit's hallways, monkeys everywhere. He said, "Poodie, I know I'm tripping a bit, but are there monkeys dancing in that window?" I replied, "No, Pooh. It's the shadow from the nurses walking by." I had to close the blinds and cut off the TV before I left each night. I knew when he was back to normal because in a stern voice he said, "If you ask me those questions one more time...!" Eventually, the fluids regulated, and he was back to his old self.

After being in intensive care for a few weeks, he was scheduled for stomach surgery to remove the scar tissue causing his abdomen's infectious pockets. Doctors seemed afraid to operate because of his physical condition and the horror that had previously taken place in his body. (By this point, we had lost count of his abdominal surgeries.) But again, he survived the operation. At least ten local congregation members went to the hospital to get tested to see if they were a match to be Delmar's kidney donor. There was a match, but he was too sick to receive it. He was discouraged. He expressed to us that he felt this was a once-in-a-lifetime opportunity, knowing the statistics of the turnaround time of receiving a kidney on the waiting list.

After leaving the hospital, he was still vomiting and unable to eat and was experiencing excruciating stomach pains. The doctors operated once again and removed heaps of scar tissue from the previous surgeries.

Meanwhile, the car stopped being reliable. Sometimes, I had to leave the hospital to prepare for work, usually around 2 a.m. or later if I was not allowed to stay, and the car didn't always start. Also, I don't know about you, but I'm not too fond of parking garages, especially in the wee hours of the morning. My dislike stems from action movies I've watched on television where the victim walks through the parking lot, unaware of a predator who comes along and injures or robs them. Whenever I left the hospital, getting to my car involved walking down a long ramp to the parking garage area, then catching the elevator when it was working; if not, taking the stairs and walking through a crowded parking lot alone. I'm a big girl, but between you and me, I was scared.

Delmar was sent home with a feeding tube receiving parenteral nutrition through his neck, which served as his food and required reloading every twenty-four hours. This process meant that I had to make sure I was home in time to sterilize and change all his tubes. I was hands down the best nurse he could have requested. With a frail body, in his new altered voice, Delmar said, "Take me to the car dealership. Bishop, I must do something to ensure her safety. She has to have dependable transportation." Don't "aw" yet. He and his best friend Stanley thought it was hilarious when I told them of the last time the car broke down and I had to push the car up a hill into the gas station. They kept saying, "Poodie, tell us again." With two or three IV bags and draining tubes dragging on either side of him, a frail body of skin and bones, and a feeding tube in his neck, we went to the car dealership. I know the car salesman thought, "Let's honor his last dying wish and give him a car." We prayed, and God gave us favor.

We left there with a beautiful white, four-door Toyota Camry with a gray interior. Most importantly, it was dependable. The Lord had made a way.

A few months later, Delmar's gallbladder was removed because of severe back pain. After the removal of his gallbladder, he was still suffering from a twisted bowel. His numbers were not good, so they scheduled him for yet another operation. The doctor blatantly told him that it was doubtful he would survive the surgery, but it was a risk the doctor was willing to take. By now, Delmar's faith was the size of a mustard seed, but this is all that is required. I remember that day so vividly because I was at the salon doing my sister Denise's hair.

Once we got the news, she had me at the hospital in five minutes. She had that black sports car in the wind. When I arrived, I said, "I need to see my husband." I approached the nurse's station, explained who I was and asked to see him immediately. The nurse replied, "I'm sorry, ma'am, he's already in pre-op."

I said, "Ma'am, the doctors said he might not make it." She again stated that we couldn't go there. With my bold swag, I said, "Ma'am, you're going to open that door, and this big guy (my dad) and I are going back there."

And she complied as she was probably terrified seeing us as these two tall, looming threats. When we arrived at his bed, Delmar was sobbing, saying, "I need help. Bishop, I need help." The sound of those words made my heart crumble. Was this it? Was this the last time I would see, feel, or talk with him? Bishop began to pray. As he was praying, the anesthesiologist continued doing his write-ups, and we continued to pray. All that Delmar had been through was physically and mentally draining, and he needed strength. Delmar and I wept while Bishop prayed. I think I was sobbing and crying, saying, "Jesus." When Bishop said "Amen," the doctor canceled the surgery. Thank God the Lord had saved his life. Delmar just wept, and the terror subsided. He had cheated death yet again. On the ride home, I heard the Lord clearly say, "Learn to respond to Me and not the situation." Let's be transparent. Sometimes it's hard to believe what we know. Trouble is most times based upon a mindset. Have you ever used all your energy worrying about "What if?" In her book *Get Out of Your Head,* Jennie Allen says, "The enemy has snared us with two little words what if." "What if" leaves just enough space for doubt. Unbelief ties God's hands. He operates by invitation only. With those two little words, he sets our imaginations whirling, spinning tales of the doom that lurks ahead. Well, defeating "what if" is not surprisingly found in two other words: "because God." Depending on which two words you choose, you can spiral down, or you can take wings.

I'll be honest; I was a little lost. I was praying, but what I saw was bigger than my faith. But when my thinking changed, so did my faith. We must do a Romans 4:17 and call those things that are not as though they were.

The next day, while finishing dialysis and getting off the gurney to weigh himself, he noticed blood dripping onto the floor. To his alarm, an abscess had burst through the stitches in his abdomen. The abscess, which was to be removed during the canceled surgery, had burst out of his stomach. God performed his surgery. Doctors say it was a miracle that it burst through and didn't burst in his colon. This event was a bittersweet moment because the hole in his stomach led to him wearing a colostomy bag for over a year.

Wearing the bag consisted of skin cement and a bag with a flap that collected feces and blood. Delmar's stomach kept forming new holes, which made it impossible to hide the horrendous odor. Now Delmar was rather vain. He loved to look and smell good, so this was a doozy to his esteem. He had to change the bags so frequently that the skin on his stomach became wafer-thin. When in public, others would smell the awful odor and began to comment openly. Once, we went to a wedding, and his bag sprung a leak, and the chatter started. The comments were somewhat harsh, and there was nothing he could do. To avoid embarrassment, he would leave and go home. He shut down and became a recluse. The colostomy bag was crushing, and depression was trying to take up residence. I watched it trying to get the best of him. All he wanted to do was remain in bed. I could not allow him to give up on my watch. He had to get up. Although I could only imagine his pain, embarrassment, and shame, I couldn't allow the devil to get a foothold in his life. *If the devil can get you to sit down, he will get you to lie down, and then he will walk on top of you.* Never allow your loved one or yourself to fall into the trap of the devil, even when it seems like there is a good reason. Once the spirit gets off track, healing is a distant dream. It is your spirit that heals you with the assistance of a good doctor. Let your loved one live as normally as possible. If they cave into the sickness, the sickness will win. Keep pushing them while simultaneously reminding them of their healing. Don't welcome the illness. Fight through. I promise you it will keep them living longer.

Delmar needed help in the worst way. The colostomy bag had to be the most unpleasant part of his sickness. I can remember having steamy sex. Just about the time things were getting interesting, his colostomy bag began to leak on me and all the linen, so that was the end of that romantic interlude. We had to take care of the odor, throw away more sheets, and bathe. Understand that the odor was so strong it would wake you from a deep sleep. Whatever it touched was ruined and had to be thrown away. Delmar felt less than a man and was humiliated. He said the worst part of being sick was his loss of dignity in this way.

Matthew 17:20-21 talks about mustard seed faith. We were down to mustard-seed faith, mustard-seed money, mustard-seed everything, and we were still not out of the woods. By mustard seed, I mean almost nothing. Everything was almost depleted. He could have passed at any moment. Desperate to close the holes, he consulted with a colon specialist who told him to be happy that he was alive and living. The doctor stated that someone would have to hold a gun to his head before operating on Delmar's body again. I guess the twenty-three-hour surgery that he had just performed on him haunted him.

He then went on a journey searching for doctors who could help him reverse his colostomy bag. We tried countless doctors in the city. After reviewing his medical records, no doctor would even see him. However, we kept the faith even in our bleak situation. We still would lay in bed and have conversations about his healing and dreaming of everything we wanted. After a year, Virginia experienced the terror of the I-95 snipers. Everyone was fearful. There was a man shot, and the bullet ricocheted in his body, and the doctor on staff saved his life.

Meanwhile, Delmar's colon doctor took a job in Arizona, leaving the sniper doctor as Delmar's new surgeon. God knows how to set you up! There is nobody and no one who can hinder God's plan for your life. It's not until we are completely helpless that we know the power of God. This new doctor called Delmar in for an appointment and looked at the encyclopedia of his medical charts. He told him how he could successfully repair his colon with great confidence. We started praising God so uncontrollably. When it's incredibly dark, God will send a ray of hope. A streak of sunshine. Finally, some good news. We left that office praising God in faith, believing He had already done the work. The years of prophecy were about to be fulfilled.

As you can see, sometimes God answers prayers slowly, so we can grow in character, faith, and confidence until we know He is the source of everything we need. *Habakkuk 2:3 TLB states, "But these things I plan won't happen right away. Slowly, steadily, surely, the time approaches when the vision will be fulfilled. If it seems slow, do not despair, for these things will surely come to pass. Just be patient! They will not be overdue a single day!"*

God will always deliver what you need on time. You don't need it until you need it.

Don't rush it. A blessing out of God's timing can be a curse. In our opinion, the worst part of Delmar's healing was about to be over. God will move people in and out of your life to serve His purpose. Who leaves your life is just as important as who stays in your life. Trust God with the details. He's perfect in thought. Our work is to have faith. So many times, we want the blueprint of God's moves before we trust Him. When your promises seem to go in the opposite direction, God is still working it out. Even when we can't trace or feel Him, He's still working hard on our behalf. He just needs your trust. Faith unlocks His power. Even if we knew His every move, we still wouldn't understand.

On Valentine's Day 2003, Delmar had a successful colon reversal. That was the best gift of love I could ever request. The colostomy bag was gone, and his bowels were regular. At this point, nothing had been normal in Delmar's life for twelve years.

Faithful in Fear

As stated before, Delmar was an avid worshiper. And he was an exceptional emcee, if I may say so myself. Being the worship arts director at our church required a lot of energy. Through it all, he remained faithful in his praise. However, his condition did not change, and neither did the power of his praise. It was customary for Delmar to lead the congregation into high worship every Sunday, Wednesday, and special occasion. He would toss me the microphone during high worship, disappear, go vomit, come back, wipe his mouth, and resume leading worship and giving God his all. In his world, there was never a reason not to give God praise. No matter what was going on, he reserved praise for the Lord. *We had a pact never to give more worry to a situation than we gave praise to God.* God has a contract with us, so we must make a contract with Him before trouble makes an appearance. *The cross was our pay advancement to whatever we needed in our future.* A few times while he was sick, he would send me to church to deposit a praise. I can remember one time being so weak all I could do was roll on the floor and cry. Although a lot had happened, God had performed miracle after miracle. We were on Cloud Twelve.

I will never forget the first night he returned home from the hospital after his colostomy reversal. He could get in bed, and we could hold each other. Do you know how good that felt? Delmar just had a special touch. Lying in his arms with my head on his chest, listening to his heartbeat while he held me was one of my favorite positions. It was my pacifier for sleeping. My second favorite was when he would just hold me lying behind me with his face on mine, and we would just talk and say how much we loved each other or talk about whatever was on our hearts until we fell asleep. Holding each was our norm until we started sweating from body heat. We had true intimacy. You develop a special appreciation for the small things when the basics are gone. My pillow was wet with praise as the tears flowed. It was nothing to wake up in the morning with him staring at me. As soon as he saw the white of my eyes, he would say, "Good morning, Beautiful," and gently kiss me with his soft lips. He would then say, "You are the most beautiful girl I know." I almost believed him. Ha! We were well on our way then. We caught a long break from health scares. He was on good footing, and we had some normalcy.

ALL VOWS TESTED

In sickness and in health, for richer or for poorer. I never thought we would live out all the vows we made on October 11, 1997, but we did. I knew some of what I was getting into, but I didn't realize its magnitude. I had no idea that God was answering all my childhood prayers through my marriage. It is so important to get married for the right reasons. When we say, "I do," we don't know what that might entail. So many couples are in love with the day or the idea of marriage. For me, it was about companionship, knowing I would always have someone in my corner. I agree we must be physically attracted to our mates, but the physical will change. Muscles sag, butts drop, hair thins or recedes, and bellies grow, but love remains the same. Many are in love with the idea of getting married or the wedding day. Let's be real. Marriage is *work*. Your mate can sometimes mirror your inadequacies. Marriage is, in essence, two worlds colliding and being melded together as one. If your love is surface, it won't endure the test of time. When we say "I do," it's a loaded response to the good times and bad. It takes time to figure out what will uniquely work for the two of you. We had a unique marriage. We had separate bank accounts. We borrowed money from each other until it was necessary to put it together. We did what worked for us.

Marriage is a vow before God. In marriage counseling, we learned never to discuss the things we didn't want to happen, such as divorce. We took it off the list of multiple-choice answers. We vowed to stick it out regardless of what we had to endure.

We prioritized each other by supporting one another and not withholding anything from each other. He was the wind in my sail and, to be transparent, a thorn in my side at times. He made me believe I could do anything. Whenever we went places, people combined our names, "DanielleDelmar." People who knew Delmar, though I didn't know them, called me by my name as if they knew me, including the random pet names of Poodie and Gladys. They knew of my accomplishments, hobbies, what I liked, what new tech toys I had recently purchased, and the latest news in my life. There was nothing left for me to say. Delmar's friends and acquaintances knew about my parents, my mom's fantastic cooking and friendliness, my father's awesome messages and jokes, my sisters, brothers-in-law, and all of my nieces and nephews. They thought my sister's kids were our kids. Delmar was proud to be my husband, and I was proud to be his wife. I'm so glad I did not pass up this extraordinary man because of his physical ailments. He made me love him through his love for me. I know for a fact that Delmar was carved out just for me. He was the complete opposite of me. Delmar helped me develop the underdeveloped areas of my life. He lived life out loud while I lived life in the corner. Delmar was loud, and publicly I was quiet. He loved public affection, and I loved private affection. He was expressive, and I was an extreme introvert who mostly communicated through letters. Being an introvert and not expressing myself started causing me internal problems. I couldn't sleep, was on edge, and frankly got sick of ignoring things. I was suffocating in silence with conversations that kept me up all night, anxious, burnt out, and depleted.

Delmar, being a communicator, taught me how to speak. He wanted to hear my feelings, not read about them. When I became comfortable sharing, I talked his ear off about anything and everything. Seeing how he spoke his mind and went to bed every night with a clean heart, clear mind, and conscience encouraged me to seek peace and tell my truth. It was so easy to talk to him. If you are experiencing ostracism, rejection, slander, being falsely accused, and other types of abuse, you must understand that you need a safe place to reassemble, recharge, and refuel without judgment. Yes, there is a God who ultimately puts us back together and heals us, but we also need someone made of flesh and blood. Delmar was my earthly place of refuge. Regardless of what I faced, I could run into his arms and be loved, accepted, prayed for, defended, and vulnerable physically and emotionally. There is nothing like talking candidly and transparently with someone who totally gets you. There's no judgment, and you don't have to fix yourself up a certain way. They hear you and give you the best advice because they know your strengths and weaknesses. By nature, I am a protector. The last thing I wanted was to burden my loved ones with my pain. I never wanted my hurt to transfer to others, so all my words were protected, but with Delmar, I could say it (right, wrong, with tears, anger, or laughter). After talking with him, I would find myself laughing at what was making me cry. He had a way of turning the conversation around as he shared his view of the situation. He always reminded me of the big picture in small situations, but he did have a little thug in him. After calming me down, he would say, "Them crackheads better leave my wife alone because I will cut a crackhead on the first Sunday, in my good black suit," and we would laugh. He would then end it with "crack baby." Ha! Everyone who acted up was a crack baby. We were indeed one and had an unbreakable bond.

I'm so grateful for our path and couldn't have asked for a better partner. A best friend second to none. I was completely vulnerable, with no guard up or fear of abandonment, and I gave him full access to my heart. I trusted him completely with everything I had, including my heart. There was nothing good or bad that we held back from each other. We were so intertwined that we could ride in the car and sing the same part of a song simultaneously. It was pretty amazing! Our struggles gave us strength and caused us to become creative. This is why our communication was so strong because that's all we had in the hard times in our relationship. *We told our situations how to behave instead of them dictating our feelings and actions.* Yes, you have that power. Husbands and wives should predetermine not to compromise certain things, and for us, that was our love for God. *Every relationship needs a core value they refuse to compromise.* Having a mutual core value kept us on the same page. It's the glue of the relationship.

A few times we wanted to choke each other, but having a love for God made us reconcile before we went to sleep. I'll admit, sometimes we still had some residue, but forgiveness always won. We looked to God for everything because He was the author and the finisher of our faith, holding the answers to our difficult and extreme situations. No, it wasn't always peaches and cream. We both had our selfish periods, but love had the final say. A person must make some decisions in advance to give direction when challenges come. One of the decisions we made was never to cheat on each other and stick it out. For fun, I liked to ruffle his feathers. I asked him what he would do if I cheated on him. He would say, "Girl, don't play with me. You know I'm crazy." He continued to say, "I guess it will be you, your boyfriend, and me because I'm not going anywhere." Delmar had plenty of female friends with whom he went to lunch, and I never questioned his loyalty. Here's another kicker: all of our marriage, I had men ask me out and all those shenanigans. When he was really sick, it seemed as if the offers intensified, but I would not cheat on my husband. He was my one and only, and that was the way it was going to be. People would say, "Dani, you are strong." I am only as strong as I was weak. Love does what it needs to do to get the job done. It always looks out for the best interest of the loved one. Love finds a way. God gave me the grace to stay faithful and make it through. The devil will creep in where he can get in. Set meaningful boundaries and core values before the storm or test arises.

THE THIRD WHEEL

So, what do you do when sickness becomes the loudest voice in the relationship?

For us, sickness was our third wheel, the real bride, that repeatedly interrupted our lives. She was like the screaming child who always needed our attention and resources and was impossible to ignore. Our lives revolved around her. She made her demands, and we had to comply. She was the real test of our relationship with each other and with God. What was natural with others was a challenge for us. It was sometimes difficult, being limited, but again the struggles gave us strength. His illness affected every area of our lives. A third wheel is a mountain that interrupts and alters your life, such as a hard-headed child, a demanding job, poverty, a cheating spouse, family, sickness, or low self-esteem; that thing or person that blocks your path or freedom.

I encourage you to find a way and make it serve you. It is there to *build you, not to kill you.* Complaining only magnifies the issue. Don't allow it to stop you in any way. It's there for a reason. Resist the urge to get hung up in the "why me" syndrome. You are always a victor and not a victim. *Victims give up their power to have an excuse.* Don't allow it to keep happening to you. Like Tim Gun says on Project Runway, "Make it work!" Rob it of its power! *Live your best life in the worst of times.* Could it be the tool God uses to build a relationship with you, or is it the tool to break generational curses? Is it the tool that will bring you the life of your dreams? Know this: It has an assignment, and in most cases, it doesn't lift until that assignment is fulfilled, but you have grace for the assignment, and grace will take the form of anything needed.

Again, Delmar's and my most vital gift was our communication. We learned to have real intimacy without sex. I've heard intimacy means in-to-me-see, and that was our intercourse for over a year. We stimulated each other mentally, spiritually, and emotionally. We had an accurate picture of what the other looked like from the inside out. We talked about the things that hurt us the most and the things that brought us joy. We knew each other's dreams, fears, and pitfalls. We welcomed each other's perspectives on secrets we never shared with anyone. We were excited to share insights on scriptures and help each other study. We had full-fledged church together with tears, raised hands, dancing, and the Word. It wasn't at all strange to go into praise. We were not performers but worshippers. We were far from perfect and fell short countless times, but we strived to live a life that was harmonious with God's Word. When his dialysis kept us grounded locally, we took mental trips. We prayed with each other and for each other. At any time during the night, either of us would embrace the other and whisper a prayer, or, in my case, after having a prophetic dream, I would wake him out of his sleep and say, "Pray!" He was always Johnny on the spot. We discussed what we admired about each other and what plucked our nerves. We may not have been able to have intercourse over long periods, but that never stopped us from being intimate. We were not embarrassed to do anything in front of each other. We would even burst out laughing during sex if something was funny. We knew each other better than anyone on Earth. Even if we were in a crowded room, we could have a conversation without uttering a word. We had our recipe, and it was working. The third wheel of sickness helped me cultivate a thriving, loving, intimate friendship and relationship with my husband and God. *What could have driven us apart actually bonded us together.* I found healing in affliction. I am so privileged to have been loved fully and grateful for that.

Maybe you have given up on love. Perhaps you are the opposite of us, and now your relationship is just about sex. Maybe you feel like you are married to a stranger. You may go outside of your marriage to express your real concerns in fear of rejection. Perhaps you are cosigning on things you don't like or agree with or on unacceptable behaviors. Maybe instead of receiving love, you are still working for love in your relationship, trying to be perfect to be accepted. You can restore the disconnect and have a passionate transparent relationship. Yes, it's going to take some negotiating and for some, counseling. I challenge you to do my personal chase challenge. Here are some tangible ways to improve your relationship and take it to the next level:

- **Stimulate them intellectually until sex is only the culmination of your intimacy**. Rekindle the love, reconnect, and rediscover the attraction and passion you once had for each other. Communicate clearly, transparently, and often. Pay attention to the conversation's tender spots, excitement, body language, and evasive topics.
- **Go deep**. Decide you are going to make it work and fight for love. Don't just coexist with each other. Become *one!* Don't become roommates. Watch and listen even when they are not talking. Find out what makes them smile and what makes them feel special. Be careful not to judge from your point of view. Remain open-minded, get understanding, and be patient with the change you want to see. You are the face of your spouse. They can make you look good or bad. Remember that our mates often reflect the areas in our lives that we hate about ourselves or refuse to deal with. The truth is the truth.
- **Ask the hard questions; find out their likes and dislikes without taking it personally**. This may sound

deep, but for the first few years of our marriage, I would randomly ask Delmar if he was healed. Of course, he looked at me like I had four heads, but his healing was important to me. Eventually, this question led to things and situations that impacted our lives. Once the seal was broken, all the worms popped out, and communication became our strength. When you love someone, you want the absolute best for them. Wherever there are holes, goodness leaks out. Everything said is filtered through the pain of the past. Two whole people is the goal.

Also, ask them what they love about you and how you can improve yourself. Find out their spots and how you can stimulate them sexually and intellectually. Pay attention and communicate about everything!

- **Heal from your scars** so you are not misdirecting them at your spouse. Figure out if you are speaking from the standpoint of scars or scabs. Scars are issues in our past that have been dealt with and made us grow. Scabs are fresh. They are open wounds that have not been attended to and are susceptible to infection. How are you dealing with your relationships? Is it from a scar disposition (healed) or a scab disposition (injured/still festering), making everyone into the person that hurt you? Stop rehearsing the past. If you are going to stay with your mate, even after trust is broken, then your decision to stay releases them from the incident. Move forward. And if you are hurting from past relationships, your spouse is not the person who did you wrong. Become vulnerable to love and grow. Love hard without reservation. Deal with issues as they arise, and not in heated arguments. Let your mate in. Withholding is not the answer; withholding builds walls in communication and is a loophole for eyes to wander and outside invasion. Take a vacation to discuss topics that are not received. *When* matters as much as *what* is said. Environment makes a difference. Don't allow matters to die in plain view. Inquire about their health, healing, and salvation status. Remember, love looks out for the benefit of others. I loved watching Delmar worship. On his worst days, when he felt horrible, he would sing, "You're a Good Good Father." Knowing how he felt made me admire his push and sincere worship. It was heart-touching and attractive.

- **Have a romantic date for $10 and make it memorable**. Make it personal by crafting what you would typically purchase to create a beautiful atmosphere. Be spontaneous and creative!
- **Create a marriage recipe**: Agreements by which we choose to live (core values, non-negotiables, boundaries, dos and don'ts, celebrations, children, etc.). Don't forget to include God. Post your Agreement in a pretty way in your home. Expectations are important; the clearer they are, the better they can be adhered to.
- **Don't become stale and predictable**. Always have an element of surprise and spontaneity (hair, make-up, outfit, atmosphere, meal). Keep yourself looking attractive. What color does he or she like to see you in? What is his or her favorite fragrance? You may not be able to do this all the time, but give him or her a "Yes Day!" Create a bucket list.
- **Send them a meaningful text in the middle of the day that makes them blush**. Tease them so bad they come through the door ready for a romantic evening or at least with a big hug. Continue the chase and never forget the things you did to win your spouse's love and continue.
- **Make time for what's important: each other**. Make time! Even when it's not your preference, act like it.

> Seeing the smile on your mate's face is your payment. Schedule an uninterrupted time and make it enjoyable. Remember, great results come from negotiation.

I could go on and on with substitutes for sex and intimacy. Your relationship with God and with each other will be your largest investment. Everything else in life is the profit from cultivating these two relationships.

Hope is the anchor of our faith. Discouragement rushes in after long-term hardship. In our case, it was sickness. In your case, it might be financial challenges, the pain of being on your own, natural and spiritual stagnation, or abuse. Whatever your situation, hope gives you the courage to keep going. If not careful, the voice of discouragement will drown out the voice of God. Sometimes it feels like when God speaks, things worsen, as in the case of Moses and the Israelites. With each plague, things got worse for them and the demands became greater. It seemed as if God was their enemy. Discouragement's voice is loud. But God is always present in every struggle. Psalms 46:1 AMP reminds us that God is our refuge and strength [mighty and impenetrable], a very present and well-proved help in trouble. When your struggle is constant, discouragement heightens.

I'll admit it can get tough believing the invisible when you're staring at your reality every day. I encourage you not to throw away your confidence. Get up every day and say, "It's getting better." My father, Bishop James F. Harris, tells us that "our words frame our world." We create better outcomes when we speak just like God. Be careful not to give the devil the weapon to destroy you through your language. Watch your mouth. We can't afford to voice our feelings because our feelings lie. Chances are there has been trauma and your subconscious mind is controlling your conscious mind. Talk your way out! Keep the prize at the forefront of your mind. There is a creative force in our words. *Don't speak what you don't want to possess.*

James F. Harris says, "We need to watch our mouths because we may be helping Satan form weapons against us." We design weapons and limitations with our mouths." Satan only knows what we reveal. You could be creating something you can't handle and giving Satan leverage in your life. We must talk about the truth and make our fears obey our faith. Consider feeding your faith and starving your fears. Sometimes, we prefer a physical opponent rather than an internal opponent. The inner bully is with us at all times. It can speak while we are smiling and even laughing, but internally, it is wreaking havoc. We can be our worst enemies according to what we entertain. Whatever we allow our minds to dwell on will eventually consume us. Proverbs 23:7 KJV states: "For as he thinketh in his heart, so is he."

Everything comes to us in seed form. We make things grow or shrink through meditation. If our problem remains our chief thought, it will grow until we feel our prayer requests are unattainable. So many of us treat our pain and trouble like a premature child. It comes in small, early, and by surprise. We give it our full attention with around-the-clock care and with access to every area of our lives. We baby it, spoil it, sleep with it, feed it, rock it, allow it to wake us up in the middle of our rest and happiness, allow it to interrupt our agenda, allow it to drain us, define, persuade, and dictate who we are, and have its way. The pain becomes our god and has the first and last word in our peace. With our mouths, we claim to wait on God for healing, but deep down within, the pain has become our excuse. It is our go-to excuse not to heal and be who we are called to be. We allow it to have temper tantrums in our belief system. It steals time we have not even lived, including the present moments. Every day we allow it to rule, it gets stronger and more demanding. What the devil does is whisper in your ear and stare you in your face for a reaction - without you saying a word. Remember this, you have options and where you are today is the sum total of your belief system.

Worry is like a weed. The Old English root from which we get our word "worry" means "to strangle." If you have ever worried, you know it does strangle you! Worry has definite physical consequences: headaches, neck pains, ulcers, and even back pains. Worry affects our thinking, our digestion, and even our coordination.

From the spiritual perspective, worry is wrong thinking (the mind) and wrong feeling (the heart) about circumstances, people, and things. Worry is the greatest thief of joy. It is not enough for us, however, to tell ourselves to "quit worrying" because that will never capture the thief. Worry is an "inside job," and it takes more than good intentions to get the victory. The antidote to worry is the secure mind: "And the peace of God ... shall keep [garrison, guard like a soldier] your hearts and minds through Christ Jesus" (Phil. 4:7 KJV). When you have a secure mind, the peace of God guards you (Phil. 4:7), and the God of peace guides you (Phil. 4:9). With that kind of protection, why worry? If we are to conquer worry and experience a secure mind, we must meet the conditions that God has laid down. There are three: right praying (Phil. 4:6-7), right thinking (Phil. 4:8), and right living (Phil. 4:9).

Worry is the advance interest you pay on troubles that seldom come. Vance Havner puts it like this: "Worry, like a rocking chair, will give you something to do, but it won't get you anywhere." Dr. William Sadler wrote that "the only known cure (for fear) is faith." What are your worries? Are you most likely to worry about something that is happening or something that could happen? If not dealt with properly, it will grow out of control until it chokes out all the good. On the other hand, if we meditate on Scripture and God's goodness and unfailing character, we magnify Him, causing our problems to become smaller.

Praise God as if the work is complete. In other words, before you see the finished product, give God the credit. Believe to see. Faith is the substance. It is the receipt or proof of purchase of what you ordered. It consists of two things: substance and evidence guaranteeing that it's on the way and things will get better. If I promised you a million dollars and gave you a receipt with a tracking number, you would become excited immediately. Before a dime touched your hand, you would start making plans and getting excited. We can have this same enthusiasm with the promises of God. He is coming through on your behalf. *Don't mistake a pitstop as your destiny.*

Here's something else remarkable about faith; it only requires a little.

The next time you are at the grocery store, grab a mustard seed. It's tiny, yet when planted, it can produce a tree that grows over ten feet tall and its branches become so thick that birds can rest on them. It will give you a paradigm shift. We only need a little faith to get the job done. I'm so glad God has simplified things. Here's a tip: *Don't complicate what God has simplified.* John R. Rice puts it this way, "Never put a question mark where God has put a period." Don't allow your mind to build a case against God, who is your only help. When we start to add our interpretations and rules and conditions to God's Word, we delay our blessings. It's our belief system that causes us to opt out of blessings. Your belief is your reality, even if it's not true. Positive and negative thinking have the same power. Whatever we decide to think, our vision and bodies will come into alignment and find evidence to support our thinking. So, when we say, "God can't," or "I can't," or "the devil is bigger," that's what we will have. Henry Ford says, "If you think you can, or you think you can't; either way, you'll be right." Challenge yourself to remove negative words and phrases from your everyday language. There are enough boundaries in Scripture. Instead, put all your weight on God. Cancel plans B, C, P, and Z.

2 Corinthians 1:20 NOG states, "Certainly, Christ made God's many promises come true. For that reason, because of our message, people also honor God by saying, 'Amen!" The verb "amen" means more than "let it be so." It means it shall be so. It shall be as the

Lord hath spoken. (Hab. 2:4 NKJV), "The just shall live by his faith." See, it is a declaration, not just an empty statement. It proclaims that God not only can do a thing but that He *will* do it. There is a vast difference between what we believe God can do and what He will do. It's incredible how we can believe for everyone else but not ourselves. We activate His promises through faith. We find the answers our hearts have been crying out for in God. Faith gives us the courage to hold on. Spurgeon says it like this, *"A little faith will bring your soul to heaven; a great faith will bring heaven to your soul."* Faith is to believe what we do not see, and the reward of faith is to see what we believe. Sometimes, we need a mental escape from all the chaos in our lives. Faith is "to accept the impossible, do without the indispensable, and bear the intolerable" (from a quote by Kathleen Norris). Faith sees the invisible, believes the incredible, and receives the impossible. When things are perfect or bearable, our faith tends to remain in neutral or park, but when God is ready to grow us through pain, we put our faith into turbo drive.

Fire-proof your faith by keeping His Word in the vault of your heart: Don't allow the cares of life to damage your hope in God. When I think of fire-proof, I think of the fire and water-resistant boxes we purchase to keep all our pertinent and valuable information protected, such as cash, passports, life insurance papers, hard drives, certificates, policies, financial information, and other valuables that are difficult to replace. The fire- and water-resistant safe produces steam when the temperature around it gets too hot to preserve the contained information. We keep it in a safe place for easy access during times of emergency. I believe that we can have the same assurance when it comes to our faith.

- **Hide the Word in your heart:** Hiding the Word in your heart requires you to seek God for answers. Psalms 119:11 MSG says: "I've banked your promises in the vault of my heart so I won't sin myself bankrupt." We must understand that sin blocks our blessings and blinds the mind to truth. The root of sin is selfishness. We can never win by being an opponent of God. He is God Almighty! It is crucial to see sin as the enemy of our souls. Without knowing the Word, the devil can throw anything our way, and we will have no defense. It's not the 99% truth, but the 1% lie that keeps us from complete victory. It's the Word that will do the work in our lives, give us instructions, and prosper us. The Word also produces faith. Romans 10:17 NKJV declares "So then faith *comes* by hearing, and hearing by the word of God."

Hide the Word in your heart to keep you from destruction and debilitating thoughts, trust God's motives, resist the devil and all his tactics, know your rights, and obey His Word.

"Our faith is really and truly tested only when we are brought into very severe conflicts, and when even hell itself seems opened to swallow us up." -John Calvin

- **Trust God's Motives:** Many blame God for everything evil and give Him no credit for daily blessings. When things go wrong, we resort to blaming to cope with our situations. Do you believe it's possible to wholeheartedly serve someone you can't trust? Well, it isn't. If we don't trust God, we will never give Him complete control of our lives. We will never find joy and fulfillment in our relationship with Christ. We will continue the defeated cycle of relying on our own abilities to get the job done. It's normal for man to want to be in control because we were made in the image of God, but even God had to give up control when going to the cross. In Luke 22:42 He surrenders control when He said, "Father, if it is Your will, take this cup away from Me; nevertheless, not My will, but Yours, be done." Real faith believes in what it cannot control. Real faith surrenders control of the situation to the able God. What price have you paid for your distorted view of God? What price have you paid trying to control everything? How long will we continue in failure? Everything God does is right, and He does it the right way. He loves us with an everlasting love, and everything He does is motivated by love. Although we must endure hard times, it builds our faith, endurance, understanding, and love for God and others. Test yourself by your actions. Your actions manifest the true desires of your heart, not your words. Any thought that dominates your mind more than the Word of God is an idol. Sometimes we are not even aware when we have spiritual temper tantrums. Our lips say we trust God, but our actions say, "God, I'm not giving you what you want or deserve until you give me what I asked for." Many then go on a sinning spree and use the excuse of being human. Sin is never justified. And if we are not careful, we will enter into self-righteousness and idolatry and call it faith. Remember this: we don't always want what is good for us and we don't always know what we need. Real faith allows God to make the decision of what is best, even when it's contrary to our request. Faith in God's Word activates His power and promises. Trusting God's motives is vital in fire-proofing our faith because our box is left open for destruction without it.

- **Resist the devil:** Would you tell a robber where to find your safe deposit box and give him the keys to steal from you? Absolutely not! James 4:7 NASB states, "Submit therefore to God. But resist the devil, and he will flee from you." The first part of this verse says to submit to God. It means to humble my opinions, outlooks, and judgments before God. It says, "God, Your word is right!" even the parts I don't understand. Then we come to resist the devil.

We cannot resist the devil if we don't submit to God and His authority. Understand that the devil is real. He is not interested in renting space in our lives. He wants to own us. He is not satisfied with conversation, negotiation, or flirtation. Remember, a good run is better than a hard fall. The Bible says to resist the devil. That means don't give him room, a voice, or authority to speak, accuse, tempt, or move you out of God's presence.

- **Know your rights:** In case of an emergency, we store important things in a safe place so we can quickly get access to what we need. We need to show proof of ID to access some items like our bank accounts and policies. In the same way, the Word gives us a road map for life, educating us on our identity and our abilities, strengths, and weaknesses. It reveals the authority we have in Christ. It gives us strength, insight, and overcoming power to weather any situation. It's God's contract with us. Hosea 4:6 KJV states, "My people are destroyed for lack of knowledge." We waste unnecessary energy, time, and precious life when we don't know our rights. Veering away always leads to destruction. We will find ourselves succumbing to things we are to rule over. We become criminals without a lawyer, helpless to defend ourselves. So, knowing our rights will help us remain free and innocent and keep us from exposing ourselves to unnecessary tragedy and curses.
- **Obey His Word:** Obedience is the highest form of worship. We must decide to obey His Word before we embark on any Kingdom assignment. We must not use human reasoning to escape His instructions. What He says becomes life. There are times when this is difficult. Loving your enemies is hard when you are innocent, and forgiving seems impossible when someone is maliciously

evil. Paying your tithe seems impossible when money is tight. Still, He knew all of this before He put in the orders. God is always testing our obedience. Obedience is the test of love and faith. *Obedience to His Word will secure the lock on our fire-proof boxes, provide protection from theft, and ultimately give us a shortcut to the life of our dreams.*

- **Maintain an attitude of gratitude:** Things could always be worse. Having a heart of gratitude magnifies the good and minimizes the problems. Gratitude allows God to expand and increase what's already there and open our eyes to it.

    Fortify your faith with these fire-proof tips and watch how God blesses your socks off.

Regardless of how long the night is, the darkness must give way to the light. Despite how long it takes, hold on to your receipt. This postponement is just the refueling station for something greater. Show your receipt when the devil tries to accuse God of being a liar. Who do you say God is? Do you judge Him as mean, critical, unfair, unjust, and harsh? Our picture of God will make us run to Him or from Him. Let's do a pulse check. Where or who do you run to in times of trouble? That's probably the God of your life. Every time we put our full trust in God, we put His reputation on the line. Be honest with God and others. When experiencing discouragement, it is essential to be candid with God and tell him how you feel, share all your frustrations and pain, and give Him back His Word. He can't fix what you don't give him. He will never barge His way into your life. He is waiting for your invitation. Have you invited Him in? He already knows your heart; invite Him into your situation. Your response is an indicator of your trust and maturity. Who do you say He is?

THE BATTLE FOR NEEDS

Having sickness as a third wheel presented several challenges. My husband had his view from the bed and I had my view as a caretaker. Our daily schedule was as follows: run to the hospital, change bandages, pay bills, and fight to believe for the better. The truth is we had to fight for everything. Fight for our survival, fight for our relationships, fight, fight, fight. As a caretaker, you are constantly making crucial decisions, carrying the weight of the now and the future, putting yourself on the back burner, ripping and running, privately crying with unanswered questions, worrying about the health of the loved one, wondering if today is going to be your last day with your loved one and the constant stress of trying to figure it out all while your mind and body are screaming for a break. Many times you are conscious while the patient is sleeping or unconscious receiving every blow in real time. One night, Delmar and I had a conversation about the status of our marriage. When under constant stress as the primary caregiver, we can sometimes get lost in the "doing" instead of "receiving." The caregiver must put the needs of the sick loved one ahead of their own needs. Don't get me wrong, I understood what he was going through, so I excused my needs for his. But when the sick loved one can reciprocate, they should. Subconsciously, new patterns are being set in the relationship. Be sure you are not rewriting the narrative of your relationship by excusing everything.

I refused to just coexist. I explained that I felt depleted because I wasn't receiving from him like I was giving to him. I get it! When you don't feel well, you don't want to be bothered, but he was still my priority when I didn't feel well. Understand that if you care for a loved one who has been sick for an extended period, he or she can become selfish. He or she can easily forget that their spouse or caregiver has needs of their own. The demands of caring for him and his life had taken a toll on us. The only thing he wanted to do was go into the bedroom, watch TV, and sleep. That wasn't working for me. I wanted to talk, cuddle, and have fun, at least some of the time. Some nights I felt so frustrated I could have picked up the whole house and thrown it into the woods or run away. I started to feel cold toward my husband. That night we had a heart-to-heart about how I felt cheated of his attention, gratitude, and affection, and Delmar apologized and assured me that he would do better.

All of me wanted to believe him, but I had that gut feeling that we would have the conversation again. It didn't matter if I had to keep repeating it. Speaking about it was my way of sharing my expectations. Instead of giving him my famous silent treatment and making him guess what the problem was, I told him, and we were able to grow from the experience. Communicating your needs is your responsibility. If you have not verbalized them, your mate or person you care for is not responsible. Not allowing thoughts, feelings, and offenses to pile up in your heart requires clear communication. Don't wait for everything to pile up and explode. Deal with issues as they arise in a loving but clear way. Withholding communication creates pockets of doubt and leaves your partner up to their own interpretation of the other's motives.

It takes more than sex to maintain a healthy relationship. You should not be afraid to communicate anything with your mate. The goal is to become one. Whether right or wrong, communicate lovingly and respectfully to gain understanding and remain open to their perspective. I'm so glad I married Delmar because he was a great friend first. I'm glad that sex was an added benefit to our relationship. Even though things may not go as you hope, communicating your needs is essential to a healthy and ongoing relationship. Love is the foundation for overcoming anything.

Here are a few more tips if you are a caregiver, provider, pastor, or anyone who constantly pours into the lives of others:

- **Take time for yourself.** Before you reach the "burnout phase," take some time to just breathe. Get your nails done, watch a movie uninterrupted, sit in the park, relax, and take time to just breathe and reflect. It's not going to be easy and guilt will try to fill your heart, but make time for you. You don't want to fall into bad health. Your life still matters in the process. You can't pour from an empty cup. You also don't want to pour bitterness, regret, and blame for the things you allow.
- **Find someone or a service you can trust with your loved one.** You can't do this alone. Ask family members and friends to help, or hire a service that you are comfortable with. Listen, if you kill yourself, where will that leave your loved one? YOU need someone. Don't allow your pride or your pretend cape to render you helpless. Pride will have you in the room with your answer and leave depleted. Reach out! Say what you need to your loved one and others that love you. Ask your church to keep you covered in prayer. Delegate what you can. Get out of your head and receive or ask for help. If you're constantly pouring into others step back and see how they apply what you have already shared with them. Know when the situation is beyond you and they need additional professional assistance. Set boundaries with your time. Take note of when people want to use your time as a pacifier instead of finding real solutions. Always speak the truth in love and let the chips fall where they

may. If all else fails charge them. People pay attention when they pay.

- **Push them.** Don't allow them to fold under the pressure of sickness. Keep life as normal as possible. Take note of their moods and emotions. Pray against those dark spirits of depression, suicide, complacency, frustration, death, and pity. Fortify them with the Word and positive affirmations. Remind them what life will be like when they get well. Window shopping is always good for birthing dreams and it's free. Don't allow their condition to dismiss them from their responsibility in their victory.
- **Let them do what they can do!** Reserve your strength for when they need you; otherwise, allow them to do what they can. We tend to go overboard and handicap the patient, member, or loved one in need. Step in when you need to. This keeps them sharp. Don't stunt their growth by doing what they can do. What you don't use, you lose. Be an encourager, not an enabler. I can't say it enough. Keep life as normal as possible. Don't start practices you can't maintain.
- **Stay on the doctors for answers.** It's the squeaky wheel that gets the attention. Research the meds prescribed. Ask about the short-term and long-term effects. Get a write-up from the pharmacist. Keep a notepad of questions and reactions you notice. Often those who are ill have several specialists and sometimes communication gets crossed. Go to those appointments so you can get answers. Besides, sometimes the patient is so overwhelmed by bad news that in order to cope, they shut down.
- **Pull on God.** Remember that God sees you and hears you. You are not alone. 1 Peter 5:7 NIV says, "Cast all your anxiety on him because he cares for you." Just throw it on Him, and let Him carry your burdens. Jesus said we could

cast all our cares on Him because He cares for us! Shut the devil up! Keep an iron-clad mind. Have something good to pull from before you need it. God's got you!

- **Keep Holding On.** Keep those conversations of healing and deliverance on the tip of your tongue. Don't speak what you see; speak what you want to see. This is just a speed bump. Remember, miracles are within your reach. Keep a good future in mind. Again, God loves all parties involved. He can peek into the future and make now decisions. Pray and ask God to help you to accept His decision. Faith over fear.

REQUEST GRANTED

In November 2003, the doctors declared Delmar healthy enough to have his kidney transplant. He had a donor available for over a year. Still, he was unable to receive the kidney due to his health conditions. Here's the lesson we learned; *God has already provided what we need, but we don't always have the capacity to receive it when it's ready.*

Giving Delmar a healthy kidney would have destroyed the new healthy kidney and caused even further damage. His abdomen was still infected. He was still running fevers, his blood pressure was still high, and he still couldn't eat. There may be things that need repairing: a heart that needs mending, a mind that needs stability, or a motive that needs to be purified before someone can receive what God has for them. One of God's hardest jobs is weighing out our troubles and our blessings so neither destroys us. In Delmar's case, they had to build a vascular system and reroute blood flow to provide blood flow to his new kidney because of his abdomen's bad condition. His stomach looked like a road map of the cuts and scars from his surgeries and traumas.

When we are healthy mentally, physically, and spiritually and the time is right, then the blessing that we have prayed for manifests. You have heard this before; "delayed does not mean denied." God is up to something and when God shows up, so does everything you requested. He is a reliable and trustworthy source who channels resources to us. Again, God doesn't need substance. He can just speak what you need. He commands, and it happens. So, if you are weary of waiting on God, hold on. He heard you. You are always on God's "to-do" list, and everything He does is motivated by love. The real question is, "What will you do and believe while you wait?"

Pay careful attention to your attitude, expectation, and your language. What is your conversation by default? Do you speak more of the pain than the healing? Or do you speak more of your bright future than your painful past? What's really buried in your heart will surface during difficult times. And, by all means, don't adjust your mindset to trouble, struggle, illness, poverty, or hurt. Fight! Don't allow a temporary situation to become a permanent mindset. Again, don't create weapons for the devil to use with your mouth. *Who you become in the process is more important than the prayer request.* The process becomes the prize.

My brother-in-law, Frank H. Wilson, an NFL player, was a perfect match. He graciously, without reservation, donated his kidney. After continuing with dialysis for a week and overcoming temporary diabetes, Delmar was in the clear. God did it! God had done the extreme. Delmar wasn't even a candidate for what he needed, but grace showed up as a kidney, and he had his life back. His outcome was not supposed to be that way, but God was there. When we should have been mourning, we were dancing. Many who were healthier had different outcomes, and some even died, but God spared his life. *You will never know your strength until you have to use it. You will never know that God is all you need until God is all you have.* Think about this: *our weaknesses define our strengths.* Think about it. How do you know you are strong if you've never been weak?

Though many view weakness as a handicap, it allows you to discover new strengths to set boundaries and limitations. It's an alarm to call for help. It reminds us that we need God and others to complete our life's mission. Weakness is a helplessness that is impossible to disregard. When we are at our lowest, we reach up and out for the answers we ignore. Let's be honest. Most of us can't receive what we need until we are weak enough and have lost the strength to fight. *Sometimes we must be disabled to be enabled.* As long as we can handle it, we remain self-sufficient and self-reliant. In those times, we run to God to be our Savior and our strength. Paul says in 2 Corinthians 12:8-10 AMP: "**8** Concerning this I pleaded with the Lord three times that it might leave me; **9** but He has said to me, 'My grace is sufficient for you [My lovingkindness and My mercy are more than enough—always available—regardless of the situation]; for [My] power is being perfected [and is completed and shows itself most effectively] in [your] weakness.' Therefore, I will all the more gladly boast in my weaknesses, so that the power of Christ [may completely enfold me and] may dwell in me. **10** So I am well pleased with weaknesses, with insults, with distresses, with persecutions, and with difficulties, for the sake of Christ; for when I am weak [in human strength], then I am strong [truly able, truly powerful, truly drawing from God's strength]." This means, God, when I have run out of myself and become totally dependent on You, that's when I'm strong. *Weakness exposes pain to a cure.* Dr. James F. Harris states, "Sometimes you're at your best after what seems to be your biggest downfall. It's part of His plan. Nothing will happen that He can't work out." There's an old saying, "No test, no testimony." God loves turning a mess into ministry. He loves to flex! During these times of testing, He proves you and then blesses you. We must see challenges as opportunities to soar. Our perspective makes all the difference in the world. It is our perspective that dictates the story we tell ourselves about the obstacle, our abilities and whether we stay stuck or soar. Your positive outlook creates momentum. The goal always outweighs the obstacle. Our mindset determines our attitude and altitude, and our attitude determines how long we will remain in the storm. Remember, whatever He allows has a victory sentence attached. Augustine put it this way, "God gives what He demands." The writer of Hebrews confidently tells us, "Let us then approach God's throne of grace with confidence, so that we may receive mercy and find grace to help us in our time of need" (Hebrews 4:16 NIV).

Grace is unmerited favor, God's ability, kindness, and love of God toward man. (Titus 3:4) But I love this simple definition I found of G.R.A.C.E. (God's Riches At Christ's Expense). John Blanchard says, "For daily needs, there is daily grace; for sudden needs, sudden grace; for overwhelming needs, overwhelming grace." If that's not good enough, the Bible says He gives us greater grace. "But he giveth more grace. Wherefore he saith, God resisteth the proud, but giveth grace unto the humble." James 4:6 KJV. "From the fullness of his grace we have all received one blessing after another." 1 John 1: 16. In other words, when we received grace, we were given all we would need. Grace is abundantly adequate. So, if you have a terminal disease, overdue bills, an addiction, overwhelming grief, a pending divorce, sickness, or an impossible obstacle or situation, there is more grace. Grace does the unthinkable. Grace always trumps the problem. Grace becomes what you need. Understand that grace does not appear in the planning, dreaming, or sharing stage. Grace appears like a hero when there is a need. Needs activate grace. So, in order to experience the fullness of grace, you have to do something. Grace will fill every hole. It seals the deal. Where would we be without grace? In His song, Grace, Clint Brown puts it this way: *"Where would I be? You only know. I'm glad you see through eyes of love. A hopeless case, an empty place if not for grace. Amazing grace, how sweet the sound, I once was lost, but now I'm found. A hopeless case. An empty place if not for grace."*

God has left you an arsenal of weapons: His Word, His love, His life, His power, grace, mercy, and direct access through prayer. Therefore you can make it - as no force, circumstance, or problem can compete with their power. We are all trophies of grace. Lean into God and watch what happens. It's happening *for* you, not *against* you. We are to tell of the saving power of Jesus, His ability to deliver, His grace that makes a way, and His yoke-destroying anointing. How can you speak of how He brought you out if you were never in anything? God may not immediately change our circumstances. In fact, He may allow the adversity to continue to strengthen and purify our faith. *When we change, everything changes without anything changing.*

We have to take the faith fall, that fall in which we drop blindly into the arms of Jesus and trust Him to catch us. Let weakness serve its purpose to make you healthy and whole. Let it get you out of life's ditch and put you back on the road to prosperity. Sometimes you may have to stretch to use faith muscles you didn't know you had. Besides, *a faith that does nothing is worth nothing.* Don't let fear stop you from what faith brought you to. It is said that faith is not so much believing in spite of the evidence but obeying in spite of the consequences. *Understand that Satan wants to destroy the root of our hope, our faith.*

When we feel hopeless, we do desperate things that usually lead to our demise. "Faith means being sure of the things we hope for. And faith means knowing that something is real even if we do not see it" according to Hebrews 11:1 ICB. Put a NOW in your faith confession. Now I am healed. Now the way is made. Now I have peace. Now I am successful. Now I am loved. Fill in your NOW. Don't form a blockage of doubt that will prevent you from receiving. We develop heart murmurs and blockages. Our main arteries get clogged with filthy thoughts and lies until the heart becomes so unhealthy that it attacks us and prevents anything good from getting through. Just know He will bring you out. He will deliver. He heard every one of your prayers and delivered you out of them all. Just don't box Him in. He's working even when you can't trace Him. Don't just look in one direction for God to bless; look everywhere. Many have overcome illnesses in their lives with our story. Although we had numerous problems, we were happy. We chose joy. Happiness is the result of circumstances, but joy is a choice regardless of what's happening. In the middle of our worst storm, we can choose joy. There is absolutely no place that God can't reach and nothing that God cannot heal. We had our lives back. We traveled, ate at the finest restaurants, enjoyed sexual intimacy, and enjoyed life. His skin glowed again, and his energy was off the charts. Delmar made up for every day he could not eat. He saw eating as a privilege after not being able to eat for over a year. The restrictions were over. Have you ever been so blessed you had to pinch yourself? That was us. We were free to worship, praise, and experience things we discussed in distant dreams. We saw our faith materialize. God gave us a second chance at life by performing the miracle of healing. We felt like we were God's favorite couple. After all our ordeals, we walked into one of our favorite restaurants where we saw a group of doctors who had played an intricate part in Delmar's healing process. When we approached their table, their jaws dropped and they stared as if they were seeing a ghost. Yes, the case study had survived. The doctors had given up on Delmar, but God was just getting started!

We may be a little weird, but we both felt privileged to know God intimately. No one can steal the nuggets we learned during the process. We knew by experience what God could do. We had a personal Savior. No, we didn't always get it right. Yes, at times our faith vacillated; yes, we cried; yes, we felt disappointment; yes, we were tired of going through; yes, it hurt; but we were quick to get back on track by repenting and asking God to help us see the situation through His eyes. It is important to note that the same God who can heal us of the common cold is the same God who can cure cancer, diabetes, and the worst illnesses that exist, even the ones not named. Someone has overcome your condition and situation. You are not by yourself. All our trials and heartaches are the same. We all have a mountain of equal size in our lives, so don't allow the devil to accuse God of picking on you and making you think you are the only one. Yours may be financial, others may be health, others may be family and so on but to each of them, it's a huge mountain. The way of escape is right before your eyes, and the problem has an expiration date. I Peter 5:10 KJV states, "But the God of all grace, who hath called us unto his eternal glory by Christ Jesus, after that ye have suffered a while, make you perfect, stablish, strengthen, settle you." After the trial has served its purpose, it will lift, and you won't recognize yourself. Again, you need those troubles to develop properly. God must be our absolute solution in every instance. Although doctors are great and we need them, they are practicing medicine. Again, it will never be the doctors that solely heal you; it will always be your determination in your spirit to inherit what is rightfully yours through Christ. Our pain became our trophy of triumph. Question: is there anything too hard for God? My answer is DOUBLE NO! With God, all things are possible. Pause and imagine God answering your desperate cry. Now go ahead and rejoice.

BELIEVING AGAINST ALL ODDS

Yes! The pain was paying us. Life was wonderful, but with each blessing came responsibility. Delmar developed a belly tumor due to abdominal trauma that left his stomach noticeably lopsided. One side protruded at least ten to fifteen centimeters. He also had to have a stent replacement every six months, which included a small outpatient surgery. That was a walk in the park after all we had experienced.

Along with the kidney transplant came a hefty prescription bill. Delmar was on twenty-nine prescriptions, some taken three times a day, including three anti-rejection medications, which were nearly $500 each. Thank God for His favor with the pharmacist who sold us one pill at a time or what we could afford. He would bring the price down so that Delmar could have what he needed and sometimes even provide them for free. Favor is more than money.

Then there were the Disability Insurance people who came back and demanded tens of thousands of dollars because of overpayment, but the Lord made a way. Delmar was not moved at all. He just rolled with things as they came. God had healed his body. Nothing could equate to that.

Soon after, Delmar noticed his heart kept skipping, which made him feel exhausted. His heart was literally wearing him out. After many tests, they discovered that he had a leaky heart valve. After the test, they couldn't stop the bleeding. The nurses had to take rounds applying pressure until the bleeding stopped. They thought he might need a pacemaker that would regulate his heartbeat, but instead, they tried him on a prescription drug, and it worked. We continued to enjoy every moment of life together. We told everyone of the goodness of God. It had been eleven years, and things were going well with only some minor hiccups.

In 2014, Delmar received the news that his kidneys were failing yet again but kept it a secret. In 2016 he could not hide it any longer. Upon hearing the news, all the old feelings of being trapped, the memories of hospital visits and dialysis, and horrifying thoughts came rushing in. I held back the tears to be strong for him, but when I was alone, I let it out. I got myself together, put cold water on my face, and smiled for Delmar. "Time to put your big girl pants on, Danielle," I told myself. No room for sadness and despair. God is going to do this thing. Respond to God and not the situation." After extensive tests, we paid a visit to the doctor. I will never forget that day. Delmar and the doctor were face to face and almost knee to knee when he said, "You will have to decide in a few months. Your kidneys have declined since your last test."

Delmar still had a grin on his face. I then asked about his chances of having another kidney transplant, and the doctor replied, "We don't even know if he is a candidate for another transplant." What a shock! How can you form your lips to say that? Write it on a piece of paper. We continued to say what we wanted to possess, fully believing God as He had done it before.

Meanwhile, in 2017, I became extremely ill. I felt like I was having a heart attack. I was hemorrhaging so badly that I could only ride in the car by sitting on trash bags. I bled to the point I clogged my shower. I visited the doctor's office weekly to see what my issue was, and they couldn't find anything. Their only remedy was bed rest for months. I knew something was wrong and wanted answers. My only hope was that I was in God's hands. Finally, an ultrasound revealed I had fibroids, which qualified me for surgery, but the next appointment wasn't for months. As I walked out of the room, a woman canceled, and I got the appointment for the following Friday. Relieved was I.

I had a complete hysterectomy, and things went well. A few weeks later, I got a call from my doctor. He had decided to open my organs after surgery. They found cancer in my uterus and ovaries (double cancer). Before my hysterectomy, I was about to have a procedure to stop the bleeding, which would have sealed both cancers inside. The doctor stated that my bleeding saved my life. *The thing I thought was killing me actually saved my life.* I've learned that my troubles are an indication that a miracle is about to happen. The prerequisite for a miracle is an outrageous problem. *There is an abundance in every deficit.* After meeting with the oncologist, I was told that both cancers had stayed contained, which meant no chemo, no radiation, and no pills! They had no idea how long the cancer had been in my body, but both stayed contained. I can't help but think had I not made a practice of trying to think positively, the cancer could have taken me out. God is faithful. During our break from Delmar's health crisis, my mother had pancreatic and stomach cancer simultaneously at the age of seventy and recovered with no radiation, chemo, or pills and didn't pay a dime. They stated that she had pancreatic cancer for at least five years but it never grew. Where in the world does that happen? My father had three heart attacks and cancer. He also recovered with no chemo or radiation, so I had a reference point. All I could do was weep with joy! My only work was to trust God. I remembered what God had already done and built on the experience. His resume was impeccable.

Meanwhile, Delmar continued to decline. His weight dropped drastically. It was so drastic that people began to inquire about his health, and of course, Delmar replied, "God is good!" One Sunday morning, during the miracle portion of our worship service, Delmar took the microphone. And these were his exact words:

"I thank God for choosing me to go through this to bring Him glory. When I was on dialysis before, when I was sick, and when it looked like my

world was collapsing, I said and did the church thing with integrity. Still, I thank God for choosing me to go through this to bring Him glory at a different level. I know Him better, I know that He is God, and I know that He wouldn't allow anything in my life to take me away from Him, but bring me closer to Him, to be what He called me to be, to bring Him profit and glory."

Delmar began making plans for his healing. Reality hit him hard when he was unable to travel on family vacations. He became sad; therefore, Delmar organized a family trip and had the entire family vow to attend. He kept declaring that he would experience healing in 2019. Regardless of how he felt, he kept pushing through. Then something new started happening randomly in his body. He had episodes where he would lose all strength in his lower extremities, shake from his waist up, his eyes would begin to cross, and then he'd have the taste of metal in his mouth. It was as if his body was having a massive power outage. All his senses were tested at one time. I will never forget the New Year's evening when I witnessed it for the first time. He started to get out of the car and almost collapsed in the driveway, but I caught him and just held him in the driveway until his strength returned enough to get into the house. He collapsed on the sofa for a couple of hours until his strength returned somewhat. I then helped him up and held him up until the strength returned to his legs and he was okay to go upstairs, repeating, "It's getting better, Baby," and then he collapsed on the bed.

The episode left him sore for days. These episodes started happening more and more frequently. One day at work, I received a call that he had collapsed at work and hurt himself trying to get back into his office chair. Delmar carried his sickness so well that no one knew he was sick. His coworkers and supervisor were alarmed. The episodes started happening more frequently and interfering with him leading worship. He would get up to do worship and have an attack. I knew what was going on, but one of those times, he couldn't hide it. He did not like a fuss made over him. He always had a positive response when asked how he was feeling. He would proceed to say something good about God.

He had a deep love for the youth and was a youth mentor. A part of that was teaching the teen Bible studies on Wednesday nights. One Wednesday night Bible study he couldn't walk because of one of the episodes. He asked me to wheel him in an office chair to the table. No one ever knew. He was so courageous, determined, and unstoppable. We had to pull off the road several times, and I would put him in the back seat because his body was under attack. He would communicate his ordeal to the doctors, but still no answers.

Finally, Delmar was unable to hide his condition any longer. After our Sunday Morning Worship Service, one of the sisters approached him with tears in her eyes and asked him if he wanted a kidney. Delmar replied, "Thank you, but this time I want God to do it." He continued to trust the God he served and spoke well of Him in the darkest times of his life.

THE MIDDLE

I classify the middle as the desert of promise. The middle can be a tough place to be. It's the middle that proves who you are and the truth about your belief system; it's the defining point. The middle is when we are too far to go back but feel we lack the strength to push forward. The devil's mission is to prevent us from taking one more step to keep us from our ultimate breakthrough. It's his mission to sift us as wheat, wear us out, and ultimately have us as his own. In the beginning, we are enthusiastic. Our hearts are racing over the promise, and we are optimistic about that which is to come. We believe everything God has spoken to us. By the end, we are jumping for joy, screaming, "Thank you, Lord, you did it! You are a man of your word! I knew you were going to do it! Thank you for bringing me through."

In the middle, we find out how well we listened for instructions and what we believe about God. Did we listen with the intent to apply? Did we hear a clear voice give us a clear vision with specific instructions? It can feel like being caught in a storm with no shelter in sight, where the weight of the pain and uncertainty about the future can be crushing. It may seem as though the hope and belief that once sustained you have been depleted. We can be in the middle of almost anything: healing, promotion, relationship, pregnancy, or anything that we are waiting on for a result. It's the point where we rehearse everything we have learned.

Think of it as a flight attendant giving us airline instructions at the beginning of a flight. After we have taken a few flights, we tend to ignore the instructions. We think we know and we take for granted there won't be a crash, but if something were to happen mid-flight, we could perish.

For most, we are like the person who ignores the flight attendant. We have disregarded the instructions. We half-heartedly read the Word and are governed by our own opinions. When the storm hits, we are lost. We don't understand English, the Word, or the instructions. We don't know what we have or how to use it. We panic and go into survival mode. Our only result is to watch what someone else is doing, not knowing if they listened.

Sometimes, it feels like our GPS signal has failed in the middle. Waiting and time have worn us down. We can teeter between the truth and questioning if God is even real. We question everything. We wonder if we will have the faith to endure. The middle brings all your true inner beliefs to the surface. It tests your endurance, patience, faith, trust, and every ounce of strength as you hold on to the invisible, believing for the impossible. During this stretch, what we focus on determines whether we become stronger or weaker. Our relationship with God soars or crashes. *The middle is the classroom of faith.*

As Delmar and I waited for answers, we had some low as well as high times in our faith. Sometimes we felt as if our faith was on steroids, while at other times we struggled to believe. The wait for healing felt like an eternity. It seems when God makes us a promise, everything goes in the opposite direction. Sometimes, you want God to work in silence. Just do it, Lord. I don't know about you, but sometimes after the promise life seems to run in the opposite direction and bring on other problems. When what we see argues with the whispered promise, it can sometimes confuse our faith. During this waiting time, you must practice all you know about God. Hard times do not release us from obedience to His Word. *"The conditions don't change the commitment."* His word is weatherproof. Whether you are in the darkest storm or on a sunny, beautiful beach, His Word is the same. His goal is transformation and not modification. We magnify small tweaks accomplished in our ability. However, God's plan is for us to be transformed by the renewing of our minds, according to Romans 12:2. Do you know the difference between conformers and transformers? Conformers take on the shape and attitudes of their environment. The pressure from external factors controls them internally. Transformers are change agents whose lives are controlled by the power within. The valley, low place, the desert, or the middle is when we should lean more into God for direction and strength. Speak the Word and the Word only. Tell your mind what to think. Put on your poker face and push through. Push past the noise of defeat, anguish, pessimism, discouragement, and doubt into the whisper of the promises in the Scriptures. Push past your temporal vision of the situation and the bad news and rehearse the goodness of the Lord. Train your mind to see His goodness by rehearsing how blessed you are. Train your heart, and you will always make a sure landing. Psalms 37:31 MSG states, "His heart pumps God's Word like blood through his veins; his feet are as sure as a cat's." Confuse the devil. When you can't feel God or hear from Him, give your best praise. Give God a "yet" and "in spite of" praise. Praise that says, "God, I'm in this for the long haul, and I won't let go until you bless me." Ask God for instructions and grace. Grace shows up when we are at the end of ourselves.

The Bible tells a story about Abraham and his barren wife, Sarah, to whom God promised a son when he was seventy-five. God wanted to authenticate the fact that He was God. The problem was not Abraham but his barren wife. Talk about a loss of control and knowing the facts; this seemed like an impossible task. He didn't just promise him one child, but He told him his children would number the sand on the seashore and the stars in the sky. That's a lot of kids when you can't see the possibility of conceiving one. Sarah laughed at the promise because she knew her condition and age. She even tried to help God out by giving her handmaid to Abraham. They ended up birthing a counterfeit of their promise. They thought Ishmael was the promise, but God wanted to use Sarah to birth the son of promise. God wanted them to know Him better. God will take what you want and love the most to build a relationship with Him. He will call you by your deficit or deficiency to perform a miracle. A relationship, trust, and personal growth is the goal. Twenty-five years later, Abraham and Sarah received their payoff for their years of longing and pain and Sarah gave birth to Issac. Their story is often cited as a testament of unwavering faith, and perseverance and a testament to the faithfulness of God. God proved He was a God of His promise. In their middle, they grew to know God to be a God of His word with the ability to fulfill every promise regardless of how extremely impossible it seemed. "For the vision is yet for the appointed [future] time. It hurries toward the goal [of fulfillment]; it will not fail. Even though it delays, wait [patiently] for it, because it will certainly come; it will not delay" (Habakkuk 2:3 AMP).

Then there was Joseph who had a dream he didn't understand. Genesis 37:6-11 NIV: "**6** He said to them, 'Listen to this dream I had: **7** We were binding sheaves of grain out in the field when suddenly my sheaf rose and stood upright, while your sheaves gathered around mine and bowed down to it.'" Then in verse 9, "he had another dream, and he told it to his brothers.'Listen,' he said, 'I had another dream, and this time the sun and moon and eleven stars were bowing down to me.' **10** When he told his father as well as his brothers, his father rebuked him and said, 'What is this dream you had? Will your mother and I and your brothers actually come and bow down to the ground before you?' **11** His brothers were jealous of him, but his father kept the matter in mind." After sharing that dream, his brothers threw him into a pit. Joseph's mistreatment by his brothers drove him to consider and lean on God and not man. He dealt with life as it was coming.

In the middle, the dreamer was thrown into a pit by his jealous brothers and then sent to Potiphar, whose wife set him up for the fall and accused him of inappropriate behavior. This act landed him in prison for a few years. The officials almost forgot him. Fourteen years later, his ability to interpret the king's dream landed him a ticket out of jail. He was promoted to second-in-command over Egypt. The revelation and mission of the dream did not dawn on Joseph until he had to provide for his brothers. He then understood that the dream was not for him but to prepare a place for his people when they would need it most. His payoff was multifaceted. He experienced personal growth, resilience, and the development of his leadership and administrative skills. Ultimately he was able to reconcile his family and demonstrate forgiveness and compassion towards his brothers. His perseverance, faith, and integrity lead to unexpected blessings. Your "come out" will have a domino effect on those around you. What will you do if God calls you to be the lead domino?

Unlike Joseph, we tend to think everything we receive is for us. But we are only instruments for His people. The vision unfolds between the blessing and the fulfilled promise as we continue on the path God reveals. We don't understand going through challenges. We question the promise: why God chose us, why things are happening the way they are, what to do, or where to go, but if you press through, the vision will unfold as you put one foot in front of the other.

Then there was Saul and David. At first, Saul was humble. He quickly went from a nobody to a somebody. He was a people pleaser who started thinking he knew what God wanted instead of obeying His commands. His disobedience led to his replacement and the appointment of David. David was the overlooked son doing big things in a small place. Here's a point: sometimes *you must be left out to stand out.* We must remember to serve in the dark as if everyone is watching until God shines His light on us. You will receive a reward for your labor. David was a teenage shepherd boy tending to sheep. When the prophet Samuel came to find the new king, David's father did not consider him until all the other options ran out. They were not going to bring him in as a candidate, but Samuel summoned him and anointed him as king of Israel. Approximately fifteen years passed between David's anointing and crowning as the king. During his middle, he had to fight for his life, serve a jealous king, run for his life, hide in caves, kill a lion, a bear, and a giant, and endure being criticized and undermined. The Lord was building David's resume of experience. Saul had favor, but David had experience. Saul was a people pleaser, and David relied on God. He often compared God as His shepherd in contrast with how he cared for his sheep. David was afraid to make a move without God, while Saul thought for God.

We can learn many lessons from these two biblical characters. To begin with, anything achieved too fast and easily does not last. It's in the struggle that God reveals character and motives. Our middle difficulties help us to know God. Without adversity, pride rises and seeks to take God's glory. David's hardship taught him to rely on God for everything completely. We see this revealed in Psalms 124 KJV: "If it had not been the Lord who was on our side, now may Israel say; If it had not been the Lord who was on our side, when men rose up against us: Then they had swallowed us up quick, when their wrath was kindled against us: Then the waters had overwhelmed us, the stream had gone over our soul: Then the proud waters had gone over our soul. Blessed be the Lord, who hath not given us as a prey to their teeth. Our soul is escaped as a bird out of the snare of the fowlers: the snare is broken, and we are escaped. Our help is in the name of the Lord, who made heaven and earth."

Before God can use us, He tests us. Our growth must be measured. Regardless of what we have been through, we are afraid to claim His honor when He finishes. Without struggle, we would be just like Satan, self-absorbed, self-reliant, trying to steal His glory. *Trouble pivots us back to grace.* Romans 5:3-5 AMP says it best. "And not only *this,* but [with joy] let us exult in our sufferings *and* rejoice in our hardships, knowing that hardship (distress, pressure, trouble) produces patient endurance; and endurance, proven character (spiritual maturity); and proven character, hope *and* confident assurance [of eternal salvation]. Such hope [in God's promises] never disappoints *us*, because God's love has been abundantly poured out within our hearts through the Holy Spirit who was given to us."

Then there was Jesus. His middle was an excruciating, humiliating blood bath. He relinquished divine glory to walk among us as a model of love and sacrifice. In the face of relentless opposition, betrayal, and brutal persecution, He bore the weight of our sins, enduring scorn, suffering, and ultimately death. Yet, from the darkness of the tomb, He emerged triumphant, with power beyond measure. His ultimate reward is our salvation, offering us the opportunity to embrace the fullness of His purpose and truth. As foretold in Isaiah 53, he bore our griefs and carried our sorrows, wounded for our transgressions, and by his stripes, we are healed. You are the divine payoff for the unfathomable pain he endured, a living testament to his boundless love and grace.

God chooses an impossible time to make you the biggest promise. *Often, our biggest blessings come designed as wrecking balls.* During those times, it is crucial to be intentional about meditating on the Word of God. Fill your mind with promises and empowering scriptures. Ask God to open the eyes of your understanding and allow you to see what's hidden in plain view. Remember to speak what you want to possess not your feelings or what's trying to dominate your vision. Give God credit for bringing you out before you come out, and remember that all of God's moves are motivated by love. But don't you worry: God always downloads fresh grace, power, mercy, and new wind in your sail to get you through the day. Don't quit! Get your prize! You are closer to the finish line than the starting line. There's too much at stake. There's a payoff for everything you've endure. And remember, the finest of steel goes through the hottest of fire.

GOD'S GOOD VERSUS OUR GOOD

GOD'S GOOD VERSUS OUR GOOD

God's answers to prayer don't always look like our answers. *Prayer does not guarantee that we get what we want but rather what we need.* What do you do when your dreams do not align with God's plans? There were so many things we wanted as a couple that we just didn't get. As stated before, what came easy for others was an all-out gladiator battle for us. We had plenty of times when we made good money only to have it sucked up by medical bills. I know without a shadow of a doubt that we would have raised a God-fearing child. He or she would have been drowning in our love. But after being married for several years, we discovered Delmar couldn't have children. I could have all the kids I wanted.

At one point, I experienced everything a pregnant woman experienced. That's how bad I wanted a child. I took several pregnancy tests, not knowing that Delmar could not have kids. It was all mental. We were able to help raise many children. I came to terms with not having a child one night as I walked up the hospital's long entranceway. I thought, "God, a child would have pushed me over the edge dealing with all this." And I'll never forget praying this prayer, "Lord, thank you for not giving me what I wanted." I saw at that moment that God did what was best for us, and I love Him for that. God sometimes makes decisions for our lives with which we disagree that seem unfair. Occasionally, we assess our lives and tell God, "Whatever I did to you, I'm sorry. Can I get out of punishment?" After our waiting season ends, we discover His love and protection ordering our steps.

God made another life-changing decision on Monday, January 7, 2019, and everything changed. We were having our usual praise-and-worship and choir rehearsal. Delmar came in around 5:00 PM bright-eyed and bushy-tailed, laughing and joking. Seeing him with high energy and making jokes was a joy, especially after our morning tiff over not pulling the sheets tight enough. We proceeded to go upstairs, and I began to share an ordeal that had just happened. It was trivial and crazy, and as usual, he yelled, "Now, isn't he a crackhead!?" and the conversation turned to laughter. It was nearing the time for rehearsal, and he then stated that I needed to go and open the doors for the praise team members. He started to get up, but his legs wouldn't allow him to stand, so he said, "I'll be in a little later." I noticed his breath was very acidic, which was a sign that his levels were off, but we were not alarmed. I gave him some Tic Tacs and said, "Look, you just chill tonight since you're not feeling well." In retrospect, that same night, when I went into the sanctuary, the Holy Spirit led me to get the big bottle of oil from the pulpit and pray over each instrument. Amazingly, everyone was late that night. When I finished anointing the last instrument, the team started to arrive.

I had no idea what was in store. We got through praise-and-worship rehearsal great. I noticed Delmar was still not in the sanctuary, so I gave him a call on my cell phone. He answered, but the phone hung up. I proceeded to begin choir rehearsal, and as I was teaching the song, something yelled at me in my subconscious, "Go see about Delmar!" It was undeniable. I sent my nephew to check on him. He came back in minutes and said his head was down. I knew something was terribly wrong. I dashed to my office only to find him slumped over where I left him, but I noticed he had saliva on his shirt. I began to shout his name, but there was no response. I lifted his head, and he muttered with his last breath, "I love you!" that was it. I couldn't stop shouting his name. I remember screaming, "No, no, no, no, no!" My chest got cold and my breath short. I ran back to get my phone. This time my sister and other choir members followed me. I was trying to keep it together. It seemed as if that office was miles away. My sister and I kept talking with him while my nephew Tre just fell apart screaming. We were all in shock. My niece Lauren kept it together long enough to call 911. The paramedics arrived and began working on him. I remember looking up, and I saw that he had urinated in the chair, but I still expected him to pull through. They worked on him and worked on him (Pump, pump, pump, beep, pump, pump, pump, beep). It seemed like an eternity. Being the photographer I am, I snapped two pictures. I said, "He's going to need these when he pulls through for his testimony." I felt like my faith was invincible, even with tears in my eyes. Besides, we had been here before on numerous occasions. The lead paramedic then asked for me by name, pulled me to the side, and explained that they had given him strong meds and still didn't have a heartbeat. With a puzzled look on my face, I said, "What does that mean?" He replied, "We will do the best we can."

At that point, I broke down crying on my sister's shoulder. She reassured me that everything was going to be all right, saying: "He always pulls through."

I arrived at the hospital, where a social worker came out and asked for information. I noticed she didn't ask for his insurance card. I said, "This is not good!" I was prepared to see him on a respirator. I will never forget it. My dad, mom, and I were all stuffed together in a small room with chairs everywhere.

Four friendly doctors came in and asked how we were doing. Then, the whammy. "Well, Mrs. Branch, we did all we could."

I screamed, "What do you mean you did all you could do?" They said he'd passed about forty minutes before he arrived at the hospital. I completely lost it. I wailed, crying in my dad's arms, and he just held me. I kept saying, "I can't talk to him anymore." I remember crying until I had a migraine. I asked, "What caused his death?" They replied, "A massive heart attack." They said his potassium levels were too high. I screamed again and said, "Did he suffer?" The doctor replied, "No." "I need to see him." They answered, "Wait right here while we prepare him."

Meanwhile, my mother shared with the friends and family in the waiting room, "Well, he's gone." There was no gentle way of saying it. Some fell out on the floor, some screamed, and others just cried. The nurse and bystanders also started to cry and give their condolences.

By then, his body was ready for viewing. I was the first one back. I have never seen a person in so much peace. He looked as if he was going to snore at any moment. Slowly, people began to come back and rotate out. I just kept feeling him. He stayed warm the entire time I was with him. I just sobbed and sobbed. His mother, aunt, and uncle arrived unaware of his passing. My mom had to break the news. When she told his mom, the strength left her legs and two choir members caught her. She came back, and we cried and cried. Everything else was a blur.

I arrived home and went straight to my bedroom. My head felt as if it were going to pop from crying. I could not sleep a wink. All I could do was cry and cry and cry and cry, and the tears wouldn't stop. My eyes were swollen shut. I didn't know how to feel. I was a stranger to myself. Looking around the room was challenging. Because Delmar was so systematic, I could still see him moving around the room doing his evening routine. I laid on my side of the bed, looked at his side of the bed, and wept uncontrollably. I start to rub his side of the bed and grab his pillow to smell his cologne. I still couldn't conceive that he was gone. I looked in the closet and saw all his clothes and his large blue pillbox on his nightstand. I said, "Lord, you can still raise him." I waited by my charged cell phone for someone to call with yet another miracle. Then his dialysis alarms sounded, which was a reality check. But then the ultimate call from a hospital representative who asked, "Mrs. Branch, where would you like your husband's body to go?" At that point, I knew it was a wrap. I went even lower at that point. I embraced his favorite hoodie, buried my head, and cried and cried and hugged his things, trying to feel his touch again and it started all over. I realized he was gone. I said to myself, "He's gone! He's gone! He's gone!"

I literally sat up for two and a half days without a wink of sleep. My mother called the doctor for sedatives. As sleep-deprived as I was, they didn't work. The most potent sleeping pill on the market with an increased dosage was no match for my grief. I was still waiting for Delmar to bounce back. Thinking ahead caused the pain to intensify. My main question was, *how? How* was I to live without him? *Who am I? What's my role? What am I to do? How* would I walk into our favorite spots, especially when our picture was on the wall as legendary guests? I couldn't conceive of being on this earth without him. I was handicapped in some ways because of the things he did for me and the vast knowledge that he shared. I hardly ever had to drive. I never needed Waze or MapQuest; I had Pooh. All he needed was a landmark or a side street name, and he could guide me to my destination. I don't know about you, but when that person "gets everything about you," you know it's rare. No one on earth knew me as he did. Where was my Pooh Bear? I know he did not have to suffer any longer, and I believe he had a spiritual premonition.

How can you be so happy for a person and devastated all at the same time? He had received the best gift of healing God could offer. He never had to worry about his health failing again or receiving another bad health report. He no longer had to struggle to feel good. His bills and hard labor had ceased. How could I not be happy when he had received heaven's best provision possible? He taught me so much through the way he lived. He made suffering look like a breeze as he held on to his faith. The miracle man had earned his rest after enduring. His statement of faith that he would be healed in 2019 manifested, but not in the way we all expected. After fourteen years of dialysis and a stroke, high blood pressure, leaking heart, colostomy bag, countless abdominal surgeries, pancreatitis, peritonitis, collapsed lung, gout, twisted bowel, brain surgery, gallbladder removal, paralysis, coma, asthma, numerous blood and iron transfusions, losing his mind, kidney transplant, unknown episodes, and other health challenges, I had to remember that death was a gift for him. Think about it: everything that plagues this life he had now dodged. He had that rest that could only be given by God. He had peace beyond understanding. The weight of this life had lifted, and he was finally free from the body that held him prisoner. He had taken on every one of life's opponents and had won. Despite the domestic violence his mom endured (including being shot), he turned out to be an amazing, attentive husband. In God's eyes, he was the undefeated champion. Even when he failed, God counted it as a victory. "Death has been swallowed up in victory" (I Corinthians 15:54 CSB). But my human heart was ground to powder. The best part of my natural life and most of what I enjoyed was buried with him. I missed his smile and infectious laugh that lit up any environment. He was my everything, including my entertainment. I could share the naked truth about me with him, along with my thoughts, desires, and unfiltered feelings. I was completely Danielle and felt completely secure and free when with him. What was best for him and what I wanted collided in a world of acute pain and confusion. What was I to do with me? Why did He choose to leave me here?

What I wouldn't give for him to say, "Get over here and give me a hug." What I wouldn't do to feel his touch; I would even let him slap and grab my butt in public. I miss riding with him as he held my hand. Each time we got in the car to ride, he would hold my hand until we reached our destination, including our trips to Raleigh, North Carolina. What I wouldn't do to stare into his beautiful brown eyes, rub his balding head, feel his soft lips on my forehead and mouth, and share our innermost thoughts. I long to hear his loud laughter and his booming voice in full concert singing a song by one of his favorites, Marvin L. Winans, The Winans, Timothy Wright, Hezekiah Walker, Andre Crouch, or one of his staple praise and worship songs. I missed our intimate conversations and his support. He was so caring. His back and foot massages took away the stress of the day. If I thought hard enough, I could feel his warm embrace. Lord, I miss being one with every part of our bodies touching from head to toe. I longed to lie on his chest and listen to his heartbeat while he wore my favorite cologne, Creed. Whew! There is nothing like a good-smelling man; he could get whatever he wanted when he wore that cologne. All his dreams included making me happy. I was loved completely. I recently heard in a movie that you don't need to be loved by everyone but loved deeply by one. You can be loved wide but not deep. I was loved deeply. I was spoiled. "Lord Help Me!" was the only prayer I could pray for the first nine months after he passed.

I was completely lost. What was my significance? I went from feeling exclusive to feeling common and thrown in a pile. Am I single or widowed? Am I still a daughter in law? Who is my emergency contact? What about my name? Do I still belong to him? Am I now just a third wheel or sympathy case wherever I go? Will I ever be able to love or be loved again? I went from having a sense of belonging to feeling disconnected and completely lost. I felt I was missing my security, safety, and anchor. His support was like my safe place. I could take chances and fail because he was my safety net and didn't love me any less when I failed. Life had become scary. I felt like those prisoners in the movies on their first day walking through the prison doors, afraid of what to expect while life was screaming all sorts of insults at me. I felt numb. The only thing I wanted to do was to be with him, and yes, that could even be in the grave. Death would have been a gift to my pain. I was not suicidal, but if a Mack truck hit me or anything tragic was to happen, I would have embraced it. For the first time in my life, I felt fearless. I was not afraid of anything because I didn't care about the results. I had nothing to lose. I felt dead on Earth. Regardless of how much I cried, the pain was always still at the same level of intensity when I finished.

Nothing could reach the pain: not a yell, a cry, a scream, words, people, nothing. My body physically shook with pain, and I was unable to sleep. I couldn't care less about anything. He left me with over thirty-five years of memories. I am incredibly blessed to have been loved by the perfect guy for me. I was privileged to experience miracle after miracle. I had a front-row seat to the possibilities and provision of God, sharing in Delmar's journey as his life became the teacher of my faith. I wouldn't know who God was or what God could do without our battles. Although things were tough, they became my treasure. I locked every miracle, breakthrough, deliverance, provision, and revelation in the vault of my heart.

It was the day of the funeral. I debated whether to stay home and just remember him alone or attend his celebration service and pay my respects. I physically shook with pain at the idea of going. It felt like my pain intensified. I felt helpless. What was I to do? I got my phone and turned on the Winans' classic song, "All You Ever Been Was Good." My spirits lifted as I saw Delmar dancing and singing his heart out, screaming, "Marvin!" I put it on repeat until it was time to leave. Strength came from somewhere, and I got dressed. I had a long conversation with him. I thought about what he told me the last fifteen years of our marriage, "I prayed for your healing." I never knew what that meant until his death. He would just randomly make this statement repeatedly.

I knew from all the trauma that he would someday leave me unless God worked a miracle. Still, I'd hoped that we would make it to our sixties, continuing to make great memories.

Everything I knew about God and every rumor I heard about death came rushing in. It was a defining moment. I was at the fork in the road of Better Highway or Bitter Boulevard. I knew enough about God not to allow my mind to go dark. I had to remain an ally of God. He was the only one who could put me back together. The scripture kept ringing in my heart, "...Everything he does is right, and he does it the right way." (Daniel 4:37 MSG). I felt like I was a third party in my own experience. It was as if I was a bystander, and the Lord said what was pleasing to Himself, canceling the devil's thoughts as they would come. It was so crazy how I felt bipolar during the ordeal. I remember wanting to give up, but the Scriptures kept springing up, even the ones I didn't particularly memorize. They were protecting me. Just the thought of veering off track caused a barrage of Scriptures to come to mind. John 14:26 NIV is so true; it states that He "will teach you all things and remind you of everything I have said to you." It was like an out-of-body experience. It pays to practice before the test. It was as if God was pulling me through and cheering me on all at the same time. I had taken many pop quizzes on our journey, but this midterm exam made the difference between passing and failing. I now had to practice all that I had experienced and learned. One wrong decision could have destroyed me. I had to say them out loud so my ears could hear them and my heart could believe them. Crazy to say, but that's also a time when I had a reverent fear of God. I never thought He would take Delmar. His life meant more on earth than the grave, right? I just knew he would live because the Kingdom of God needed him. Hard workers are so scarce in ministry and truly, Delmar was a gift to the Kingdom. His worship was pure and his life was the testimony of his worship. But God is sovereign. He is God!

I should have known something was coming. The week before, Delmar went outside in the frigid temperatures and grilled all our favorite dishes. We even talked about what we would do if the other passed. That Sunday, he told many of the youth how much he loved them and was proud of them. Delmar told me the day before his death, "This year, you are going to have to carry your own bags," and we laughed.

He pushed himself to have a date day with me. We went to lunch at our favorite restaurant and went to several places, dreaming and picking up whatnots. I could tell he wasn't feeling well, so I said, "Let's go home, watch a movie, take a nap, and then I'm going to wake you up." He asked, "Why are you going to wake me?" I answered, "Just because." He said, "Crack Baby." We had a beautiful evening of rest and laughter.

After his death, I felt hopeless and helpless. As the days went on, my pain seemed to intensify. My identity continued to fade even down to my worth. What am I to do now as I have no one to worry about or support? No one to pick up behind. No one to shop for or to consult about dinner. No one to accompany me to our favorite spots. No one to consult with about how my clothes looked. (He made the most boring events a circus of fun.) No one to share my successes with. I was all alone. Life felt pointless and empty. Thinking through the events of my day was depressing. I couldn't handle life without him. What was I to do without my love and best friend? His very presence became my place of refuge. Everything suddenly required effort. "Jesus, take me, as my work on earth is done." My significance is in the grave. One day, I dozed off and in a dream, "It was all a joke," only to wake up to the reality that the nightmare continued. I knew that I needed help but didn't know what to ask for outside of having Delmar back. I had never experienced pain of that magnitude.

Customarily, I am happy waking up every day, but now I was forced to wake up in extreme sorrow. Why get out of bed and experience this vicious cycle of pain? I could feel Satan wooing me into depression, darkness, and suicide. I knew better, though. I knew if I gave him an inch, he would take my life. I didn't want to die an enemy of God, so I fought to get out of bed. I knew the voice of God, and I knew the voice of the devil.

My mom had to force me to eat. My smile was cosmetic. My family was so gracious. Delmar's death was crushing because he was a family member in every way. We would reflect and talk about our different experiences with him for hours. I was lost in an ocean of sorrow and was so tired of sobbing. I just wanted to disappear.

I went through my phone and iCloud and gathered old text messages. One message said, "Hey, just checking in on you. Give me a buzz. Love you!" I played it over and over again. Thank God for digital technology. I'll be honest; for the first time in my life, I felt there was no comeback. I felt like my heart had been ripped out of my chest. For the first time in my life, my feelings were on public display, and I couldn't control them. Grief was my master. I was weak and needy. It told me how to feel and react.

So, about grief, you don't grieve things, people, and opportunities you don't feel are significant and meaningful. I was told that you are either grieved or relieved when someone passes. The symptoms are random, and they vary. Grief has a mind of its own. It is a monster that dictates your feelings, emotions, outlook, faith, hope, mood, and other things. It's uncontrollable at times. How could something so human feel so savagely inhumane? It was like no pain I had ever felt. It was sharp, acute, and deep. It was inconsolable. It was a real internal disaster that left me so confused.

Grief is constant and I couldn't soothe mine, nor control it. It was like a bully or a monster on the loose. Nothing I did could satisfy this pain inside. I thought to myself, "Where are you, God?" I could not afford to entertain the idea that God was unjust and unfair. From the other side of the bed, I knew my baby had been suffering so much, and he had been pushing through to bring me some happiness. There was nothing Delmar wouldn't do to bring me joy. I was also aware that his pain and struggle were far more painful than what he confessed. He had this way of trying to protect me from things that would hurt me or worry me.

Then the Lord comforted me with Psalms 145:17-20a, which states, "Everything God does is right—the trademark on all his works is love. God's there, listening for all who pray, for all who pray and mean it. He does what's best for those who fear him—hears them call out, and saves them. God sticks by all who love him." What kind of wife would I be to keep him here in pain, watching him suffer? I know God did what was best for him, but what about me? Why was I left here to sift through life without my one love? It was not until I was on the phone with Tione, that something clicked for me. She said: "God didn't just do what was best for Delmar, but He did what was best for you." That statement made me think. See, God does many things with one act. He can affect so many lives with one move. He's God. Not fully knowing what that looked like, I adopted it by faith and said, "Yes, God, you did what was best for me, too." I couldn't wait until I understood that statement; I had to adopt it before a self-destructing thought filled that space. Sometimes, you must grab the words and rehearse them like a song until you can remember the melody. God knows our past, present, and future. He knows what lies ahead. Who knows what God saved him from? The week of his passing he was scheduled to find out if he was a candidate for a new kidney. Maybe a "No" from the doctor could have made him lose faith and hope. A few months after his death, Covid-19 hit the scene. Was he a candidate? Who knows if he could have had an episode and died in a tragic accident? Only God knew what lay ahead and whatever that was, He saved him from it and allowed him to transition peacefully. Isaiah 57:1-2 (NLT) states, "Good people pass away; the godly often die before their time. But no one seems to care or wonder why. No one seems to understand that God is protecting them from the evil to come. For those who follow godly paths will rest in peace when they die." I had to be OK with not knowing all the details, understanding why, and trusting God's motives.

On the other hand, some attempt to try to over-spiritualize death. There is a distinct difference between faith and denial. Saying things that sound right to cover your true feelings or deflecting will only prolong your healing process. You must face and acknowledge your feelings. Refusing to recognize those feelings and emotions is called denial. The first step to healing is knowing that you are in pain. Many Christians run from their pain by using scripture to express their natural feelings. They refuse to own them and deflect them to something else. They hide behind cliches and refuse to deal with the pain. This behavior is neglect at your own expense. I believe that the pain will manifest physically if not dealt with emotionally. The body doesn't lie, and if you are not properly grieving, it has to go somewhere. Grief will manifest in other ways, including the mind, body, and actions. As stated before, grief is a normal reaction to an abnormal event.

Refusing to deal with grief can cause stress in other areas of your life, so please pay attention to yourself. Even Jesus wept. Be human, or there will always be unresolved pain in your life and that pain will lead to a roller coaster of emotions and random acts. Pain pays attention to you when you are not paying attention to it. The pain will continue to tap on your heart. You must deal with your pain, or it will continue to make a guest appearance in your future relationships and conversations. Own those feelings. Have a face-off. Get it out! It's okay to say how you feel on your worst day as well as your good day. Don't try to over-spiritualize the situation by acting super spiritual. Just be human and be transparent with God and others. Real healing comes from honesty and transparency before God and others. You are lying to yourself and hiding behind pride if you think you can overcome traumatic situations alone. You need flesh and blood to be accountable and pray for you. While healing, be open to answers, changes, new solutions, and remedies. Be careful not to shut everyone out. The devil loves isolation. It's a tool to separate you from strength and back you in a corner with his narrative about God, your problem, and your future.

The one thing we love is time, but time became my enemy in grief. When I woke up, I'd want to go back to sleep. I was in a cloudy place that seemed to get darker and darker. When I got up, I had to fight not to go back to bed and go to the dark side of depression. Depression is so real and so is anxiety. What are you to do when you are accustomed to waking up happy and hopeful and now each day is filled with deep pain and sorrow? How was I to go on?

What am I to do? I could not get myself together. I was helpless and needed help. I needed God, a pastor, and a therapist. Yes, Christians need therapists, too! The therapist helped me to sort through my feelings and emotions and revealed what I needed to pray for. You can't read the label from inside the jar. Sometimes, you need help articulating those things buried inside that constantly plague your mind. A therapist who knows the Word of God is an angel. Get all the help you need. In a session with my therapist, I learned that the pain is more acute when you are accustomed to having someone special in your life and that person leaves, or someone or something takes them away, especially when your world revolves around them. So, there you have it. I was now emotionally introverted thinking extroverted to survive. I had to do things I'd never done, like reach outside my marriage and call for help. I would stay on the phone with my sisters until the wee hours in the morning or my sister-friend, Watts. They would help me and assure me that they were there. They would also correct or help me reimagine things I felt I would never recover from. I knew my family loved me, but there is a different love between you and your mate than you and your family and friends. I had to adjust and navigate a lifestyle I knew nothing about.

My sister Tione said something so profound. "Don't look forward; just live in the moment." This statement helped me so much. I couldn't stop thinking about the next moment, the next month, the following year, and so on. I could not imagine healing from the pain in my heart. Even certain words became triggers. I asked my therapist why the word "forever" hurt so bad. He stated, "Forever hurts because you are grieving the years you had together and the years you could have had together." It made so much sense. He proceeded to say that just because he died doesn't mean the relationship ended. The goal is to continue the relationship through memories.

Don't expect yourself to do what you've always done. It may require a few tweaks. Start intentionally doing things such as lighting a candle, eating his favorite meal, going to a favorite restaurant, journaling through voicemail, and doing something that you both enjoyed doing together. He shared that I would never stop grieving Delmar and that I needed to allow myself to express my grief.

I then understood that my grief was my grief, and it was okay. See, with me, I tried to put my grief on a timetable. It may seem that everyone is moving on, and you are left behind, but no one around you had the same relationship as you shared with your loved one. Nothing is wrong with you, so stop questioning yourself. Healing is a process. Healing looks like progress after losing a loved one. Healing looks like a mess. Every part of you becomes disjointed. There's a reason it ends in ing. That means it's a continual process. So often we want to rush out of the pain and be healed. The goal of healing is wholeness. I heard someone say that healing is not the absence of pain but knowing what to do with pain. You will never forget that person. Putting myself on this crazy timeline was an epic fail. Until his death, I had to always have it together, at least on the surface. It was all or nothing. Whether it was a game of Phase 10 or my life, it was not worth trying if I couldn't win. Perfectionism, comparison, and competition to be the best also carry a grief sentence.

Customarily, I told myself how to feel and think, just plowing through life to keep living, but his death stopped me dead in my tracks and commanded me to feel again. It had served me up a heaping dish of pain, and comfort was nowhere; I had to face and feel the pain. I couldn't push it away, ignore it, or minimize it. It was like having surgery, feeling every cut without anesthesia. Holidays, birthdays, and special moments intensified the pain. I can remember fearing the overwhelming grief of his upcoming birthday. I wanted to know what I could do to avoid the ocean of tears and lonely feelings. I wanted to know step by step what to do not to feel the sorrow, but *grief has no prescription.* There's no three-step formula. It doesn't matter how many people experience it; it takes on different forms for everyone. I wanted a prescription of steps and formulas to stay in control. Nope, it doesn't work that way. You have to feel the feelings and keep moving with as much that lies in you. I felt justified to enter and find refuge in the dark space, but I couldn't just permit myself to be depressed. I know the devil, and I know he had been after me a long time, and if I didn't keep speaking and thinking well of God, he would have me. He waits for any opportunity to accuse God and set your life in a downward spiral. Because I was in a justified situation of sorrow, he wanted to come along and hang extra baggage on my justified grief, but I didn't want to get stuck in the process. The pain became the nail of justification in my life, but I couldn't hang depression, suicide, guilt, anger, and blame on the nail. Yes, grief is a process. So many things are changing at one time. What made you laugh now makes you cry and vice versa. Many days, you must push through, or you can become stuck in the process and the pain. I was desperate for healing. Grief can shake your very core, but be careful not to permit yourself to think detrimental thoughts of God and the situation. Remember, the same effort and energy it takes to think negatively is the same effort and energy you can use to think positively. A decision is your power in grief. Here's an idea God gave me during a difficult time in my life:

If I meditate on a moment too long, it will become a period.
If I meditate for a period too long, it will become a season.
If I meditate on a season too long, it will become a cycle.
If I meditate on a cycle too long, it will become a pattern of life.

Put a pin in this. Regardless of what is going on, control your thinking. You have a choice. How you heal and where you end up will result from your thinking. Something will happen in life that will challenge everything you know and believe about God and yourself. For me, I was used to my faith fixing everything, but *what do you do when you know what you're asking for is outside of His will?* My faith could not bring Delmar back. I remember being so desperate to talk to Delmar and feel his touch one day. I just fell to my knees and screamed, "Lord, please, please break Your Word just this time, PLEASE! I need to feel him and to speak with him."

Again, anger, guilt, and blame slow down the healing process. There were times when I felt guilty for not being there when he had his heart attack. I would say things like, "Danielle, why didn't you find him a specialist? How could you leave him when you knew he wasn't feeling well? Why didn't you lay him on the floor? Maybe he could have lived longer had you cleared his air passage. What if he was calling your name? You could have done more. If you were there, maybe you could have called the paramedics earlier." My mind was filled with thoughts and ways I felt I had neglected him. It happened the way it was supposed to happen. That is just a minor detail trying to take on the form of a significant regret. Then, I had to shut my mind up because I would have been devastated if I had been there. The drop of Delmar's head and those slurred words, "I love you," traumatized and haunted me because I didn't say it back. It was rehearsed in my mind minute after minute. I literally had to tell my mind to shut up!

Moments of joy or laughter also made me feel guilty. I asked myself, "How can I smile when he is gone?" I felt I should have been sad and that happiness minimized my grief or memories, but I later learned I could have both. I began to shame myself for everything good. Then, I felt like I was forgetting him and only felt comforted when I was grieving. When leaving to go out of town, these feelings also consumed me as I felt like I was deserting him and forgetting him. On my first trip, feelings of grief consumed my mind and heart. I cried myself to sleep on the plane. Once we landed, I put on my game face so I wouldn't ruin the fun for my sister and her husband while we were away celebrating their anniversary.

For so long, I could only give outward smiles. It pained me to smile. I didn't like the attention of feeling like a dependent. Just the mention of Delmar's name caused me to sob, not just cry, but *sob.* I was so happy when I got to the point where I could smile from the inside about Delmar, but that took time.

Regarding anger, I didn't permit myself to get angry. I couldn't handle another emotion, to be quite honest. I know it's real, especially if you have a loved one who died unjustly, was raped, abused, murdered, or experienced other violent acts. Some become mad at God because of what happened. They can't believe that a loving God could allow death. Either way, you determine where your emotions will lead you. *Don't be a victimizer in your own life. Decide to let go of anything that will hinder your healing progress.* Sort through the emotion in a healthy way.

I thought I was losing it until my therapist explained the stages of grief. They say there are five emotional stages of grief: denial of the event, anger for no apparent reason, bargaining, depression, and acceptance. My therapist explained grief in days. Day one is the day it happened. He emphasized that you can progress to day three only to wake up the next day, and it's day one all over again. Every feeling comes rushing back with the same intensity, but that's normal. I remember a month after Delmar's passing, I was standing at the kitchen sink, and day one slapped me in the face again. All the feelings rushed back like it had just happened and I spiraled out of control.

Never in my life had I felt so hopeless. That had to be the worst emotion I have ever experienced. The feeling was so heavy I felt like my health was in danger. The hopelessness was coming from my perspective of the situation. I had put a period at the end of the sentence. I couldn't imagine life beyond the pain. I wept so loudly and cried out to God, "Lord, if you don't help me right now, I'm not going to be here much longer." I cried and cried, simply pleading, "God Help Me!" And God did just that. God cannot refuse a helpless child. I had reached my breaking point. And then I heard his voice say, *"But I prayed for you that your faith would fail you not."* It was so loud it was undeniable. It looked like I was losing, and yes, I doubted that I would heal, but just like Peter, the Apostle of Jesus, He upheld me. I lost my courage to go on but still had enough faith to call on God. God prayed for my strength and victory before the situation existed. The master of the universe and sovereign God was my intercessor. He prayed for the things I could not utter. The only way I could lose was to become His opponent.

A sign of healing is when the pain shortens and the happy moments get longer. This is a sure sign of healing. Resist the urge to compare your process to others around you. I believe the more open you are to reason and healing, the quicker God can reach your hurt. Remember, a metamorphosis is happening. Change is painful, and it takes pain to get through the pain.

Knowing what was normal and healthy helped me. And when you're used to living for others, this can be very difficult. And this is where I got slapped in the face: "Ask for what you need." Whaaaat? Yes, ask for what you need. If it's space, ask for it. If it's company, ask for it. If it's a lunch date, ask for it. If it's prayer, ask for it. Ask for whatever you need to get through those overwhelming moments unashamedly. I felt like I was about to have a downward spiral for many days, and I had to ask people to meet me for lunch or dinner. It helped me to think or do something different and not sit around with my thoughts.

"Why him?"

My sister Alicia repeatedly said, "Why NOT him?" "Why not her?"

I remember people walking up to me, saying, "I was upset with God; I don't understand, but why couldn't God heal him and get the glory?" I didn't have the answers to any of these questions. As stated before, I had never believed in God more than when I was standing over his body while they were working to resuscitate him. As stated before, I had full confidence that he would pull through regardless of the process. I thought he could quit his job and travel the world sharing his miraculous story, which would be the staple of his testimony. He could win so many souls for God and share hope from this experience. No one could convince me that God was not going to heal him on Earth. Boy, was I wrong. You hear me say this all through this book: God does many things through one act. When we open our minds and hearts to the greater purpose and truth of the why healing will take place. Delmar had completed his purpose and lived a full life at the age of 47. It is our belief and perspective of the pain that will cause us to heal or hurt on a continual basis. He had completed his purpose. It was now my turn to intentionally be who God called me to be. His death even had a purpose. How he conquered his sickness while he lived was a gift to the world. Numerous people worldwide were impacted and changed through his example of faith. Many began to attend church and started cultivating relationships with God. Many said he was their inspiration and talked about the days when he was extremely ill and how he would not address his sickness but simply utter, "God is good!" Others were completely shocked by his passing because they didn't have a clue that he was even sick. People believed in his God!

I can't begin to tell all the inspirational stories people shared of how Delmar handled his thorn, as Apostle Paul did in 2 Corinthians 12. His thorn kept him reliant on God. *See, all of us have a handicap in our lives. It is the thing God has placed in our lives as a human limitation to keep us humble, which turns out to be our gift to the world to show His grace, power, and glory despite our handicap.* Delmar always kept a vision of his healing. His faith became the fuel to turn his pain into power. He was able to thank God for what was allowed in his life. His life was a praise to God, and he never let his handicap limit his praise or become his excuse. Through sickness and pain, he continued to serve, praise God, and excel in all he did. Although it didn't feel good, it didn't interrupt his purpose: to tell the world about how great God was and His ability to love and provide what we need. His name meant "Messenger of Praise," and he lived its meaning. You're not a worshiper until your worship costs you something. David wouldn't dare offer God something that did not cost him something (2 Samuel 24:24). If it's true worship, it will cost you everything, but the return is priceless. God always gives more than He receives.

Worship is exalting the worth of God. His character and ability are revealed through the eyes of faith. His reputation is fail-proof. In short, worship is obedience to what God requires. The value increases when situations are not favorable. Whatever we worship, we become more like. These experiences become priceless as we see God revealed in ways we could never imagine. Every gift leads us to the giver. It was as if Delmar had mastered worship to the point of it being his lifeline. Not many people fall into this category. Today, God gets the short end of the stick because many have become self-reliant, self-seeking, self-praising individuals. Their praise is contingent on their circumstances and not the character of God. As soon as the showdown of trouble appears, they complain and withdraw from God. They hold their praise and refuse to comply with the Word. They make idols out of painful situations or lust that, in most cases, may not be good for them and then they accuse God of not being a God of His Word while still professing to love God. He then gets the blame for their situations. They first utter, "How could God do this?" Their eyes shut, and their mouths open wide with complaints accusing God of being unfair, unjust, and unloving. Again, trouble and time reflect your maturity level. You can grow or shrink from hardship. Depending on your maturity level, you can run to God or from God. I know grief can do a job on you, but I thank God that His grace didn't allow me to curse and accuse Him. How you feel about God makes a real and naked appearance in painful, trouble-filled situations. What was your last response to God's gift of trouble? It's not okay to just *say* what is right. Are your words coming from your heart? We must *live* what is right even when circumstances are not favorable. Someone's life could be won or lost by our response to God. The truth is, we signed up to be His model, so whatever He puts on you, model it well. No, I am not asking you to be a hypocrite but to be authentic and godly in your response to what He allows. Yes, your human response is default, but quickly channel your thoughts. God knows what's best. Period. Who knows, one more blow, day, test, trial, problem, or failure could have changed everything. Delmar could have cursed God or messed up like Hezekiah when granted fifteen additional years (Isaiah 38). So, in faith, I say God did what was best, not just for him but also for me. He protected us from what was ahead of us. What you have is not genuine if it has not endured testing.

My eyes began to well up uncontrollably. At this point, I had cried until every tear physically pained me as it came out of my eyes. Have you ever cried that hard? I remember saying, "Lord, I can't lose anyone else." Grief can become compounded depending on what's going on in life. It has triggers that are not necessarily attached to death. Any loss was a trigger and reminded me of my husband's absence. I was in the sixth month since Delmar passed when I suddenly found out that a dear friend had to go to jail. It was like another death. Loss is so much more than death because it requires an adjustment to adapt. Sometimes, you must grab your emotions by the collar, and with that one percent of faith remaining, say what is right, practice what you know, and believe in the Word you've practiced. Sometimes, we face situations that seem 99 percent negative and one percent positive.

Isn't it ironic how God chose almost the smallest seed (the mustard seed) as a symbol of faith: something almost invisible to get an impossible task done? I started thinking when it seemed like the odds were against me, and God was my only glimmer of hope and deliverance, that's when the most extraordinary things happened.

God loves to be God in every situation. Sometimes, He must reduce the chances so He can perform a miracle. Full dependence is the perfect posture. If it's explainable, then it's not a miracle. I began praying, "God, you know what you're doing." Unless you've been God, you can't rule God. We will never be able to outsmart God. Trust the process blindly.

On February 28th, 2019, I wasn't feeling that well, so I went to the doctor to pick up some paperwork for a bill and ended up staying for a doctor's appointment. They tested me for the flu, and...no flu. I then looked at the doctor, and tears began to shoot out of my face. At this point, I was starting to feel crazy because I was so sleep-deprived even though I was on the most potent sleeping pill they could prescribe. I proceeded to tell the doctor that my medication was not working. I still saw every hour, and I was feeling delusional. Now, physically and emotionally broken down, I burst into tears as I asked the doctor for something stronger. I don't know if you have ever been to the point where something you needed was out of your control or reach, but I was desperate.

She proceeded to ask me the magic question, "Are you depressed?" I refused to the medication because I knew it would not solve the problem. At that point, I just began to cry. I replied that no, I didn't want to do bodily harm to myself or commit suicide, but I welcomed death. I was in that much pain. She left the option of depression medicine on the table, and I just left it there. I felt the medicine would only dull my pain and that it would later come rushing back with a vengeance. I needed help to deal with this debilitating grief.

Now, I'm facing another night of turmoil and sleep deprivation on top of having this cough from hell, which gave me terrible headaches. I was desperate for sleep. Now, I don't drink alcohol at all, but I thought about getting a glass of wine to help me sleep. Immediately, I had a vision of my nightstand drawer full of empty bottles of alcohol. I felt God was warning me not to start something I could not stop. I heeded His warning.

I decided to try Nyquil. OMG! Even though I went to the bathroom every hour, I could still get much more sleep. That went well, but I started feeling a little out of sorts the following morning. I sat on the sofa and felt faint. I stood up and lost all my hearing and then my sight. I could only see white lights, and I lost my energy completely. I ended up crashing on the toilet, and the next thing I knew, I was sitting on the toilet with my head lying on the wall, trying to recover. What just happened? I staggered back to bed and tried to sleep it off. Later, I had to use the restroom, but my bathroom was under construction, so I went to the one on the upstairs main floor. My sister came bursting in with excitement to tell me about her meeting with the architect for the Hope Center to be built in Delmar's honor. I was excited but felt similar symptoms coming on again. I sat on the stairs to the basement. Then my hearing went again and then my sight, and the next thing I knew I was coming to, and my mom was slapping my face like I was a cheating spouse, and the paramedics were pricking my fingers. I was so glad I fell backward. Had I fallen forward, I could have rolled down the stairs, broken my neck, and died. From what my sister told me, I went out and started shaking. I don't remember any of it. They put me on a stretcher. As they rolled me out, I could only see a circus of lights. The sheriff, police, rescue squad, and ambulance were all there. I said, "All this!" They checked my pressure, and it read 78/55. I was a little alarmed, but honestly, if someone told me I could be with Delmar at that moment, I would have seized the deal. I arrived at the hospital after the rough, slow, and bumpy ride in the ambulance. After being examined, there was still no resolution as to why I was fainting. Now I was caught at a crossroads. My parents looked so worried; the last thing I wanted them to do was worry about me. My mom said, "No one else is dying!" I was in and out of the hospital and racked up a thick folder of medical bills. I was spending thousands of dollars trying to run from the pain inside. My physical body was aligning with my desire to die.

Day in and day out, I was on an emotional roller coaster. For the first eight months, I kept my blinds closed. At a specific time of day, subconsciously, I would go into deep sorrow. As the sun went down, so did I. I later learned that those were the times we would be together making evening plans or going to dinner. I had all types of triggers that would cause me to cry immediately: certain songs, fragrances, places, phrases, TV shows, times of day, and any type of loss. At certain times of the day, all the songs on the radio that played during the time of his funeral planning are still etched in my memory. At times, I thought he was slipping away, and I would grab something to remember his touch, voice, and presence. There was a blanket I never washed to keep his smell nearby and I kept a few bottles of cologne to remember his fragrance.

At the same time, I felt so loved. I had cards, flowers, money, books, edible arrangements, teddy bears, and gift cards coming in every day for at least three consecutive months. Then, they would come in randomly. Even now, I receive gifts on special days we shared. I can't tell you how they encouraged my heart. Even when attending church, the silent hugs brought me strength. When I got really low, I would receive a text saying, "I'm praying for you." God just kept laying me on people's hearts at the right times, even in the wee hours of the morning. It only reinforced His love for me. When I say I was a pile of broken pieces, I mean I was a *wreck*. There was an immediate change in who I was, so those prayers were priceless. The power of prayer can go where words can't reach. Prayer utters the unutterable, sends you earthly help, and welcomes God to meet you at the point of your needs. It really works! It's okay to ride on the strength of others until you can regain strength.

MIRACLES IN MISERY

I thought I knew about death until I experienced coping with Delmar's. It was crazy how things kept happening. After returning from the emergency room, I had a dream in which I told him that I went to the emergency room, and he began to cry. On another trip, I started to miss him, and when I opened the menu, his name was in bold font across the middle. For three days, I could smell the scent of dialysis in my room so strong it was undeniable to me. I started to see his name everywhere, including road signs. My dreams began to change in relationship status. In the beginning, we were married, then engaged but I would wake up before the ring. Then we were boyfriend and girlfriend. Next, I had a strange dream about us singing at a church, but I was aware that I had not seen him in a long time. I cheerfully approached him. I asked how he got to the church, and he replied, "With Michelle," who was one of our friends. I said, "Well, I'll start taking you home." With a huge smile he said, "No, I'm good." He was so happy it looked like light was coming from him. Delmar was always jolly, but this was happiness on a whole new level. I took that to mean that he was happiest where he was. In every other dream after that, we would be fooling around and teasing each other. When I asked him if he would be my boyfriend again, he would smile and say, "No, we can't date anymore." I can't make this stuff up. Now I know the scripture that says there are no works from the grave. My therapist said, "Danielle, look at it this way. God is just giving you what you need when you need it." Some days, if I was not careful, I found myself staring at the door, imagining what he would be doing for hours. I had to catch myself because it was still surreal.

The great part about our troubles was that God was always there. We both had experienced the power infused with pain and God's miracles. So many miraculous things happened in our lifetime. We saw death behave, doctors dumb-founded, health reports reversed, favor that replaced money, and more. We beat the odds so many times. Unexplainable miracles. Let me brag on His goodness right here. I remembered that I signed up for an additional insurance policy that would give me a cash payout of thousands of dollars because of my cancer diagnosis. After sharing my story on social media, a lady reached out to me and shared how she was facing a cancer report. I told her to expect God to show up in her life in the same way He did in mine. That was in 2012, and to this day, she is still cancer-free with no radiation, chemo, or pills! So many miracles took place during our healing journey. For one of those years, while Delmar was in the hospital, the company owner paid him as if he was at work. Delmar received a promotion on his sickbed. My sister Tione blessed us with a lump sum from a settlement, which paid off Delmar's student loans and some major credit card bills. We were blessed to receive a car that was given to us free of charge. When that one stopped working, He gave us an even better one. Several times, my credit card balances were paid in full and I was left with a credit. We still had shelter, and our marriage was more vibrant than ever. I also opened a thriving salon. God is a rewarder. The key is to be grateful for the small things. Have eyes to see the hand of God in your life. Never overlook a blessing. Train your mind to be thankful, and watch the small expand. Find something every day for which to give God praise, maximize what you have, and watch Him bring you increase. God will always see you through. He always gets it right.

I have responded to God with an offering in church, which caused people to feed me all week and pay for things I was trying to figure out how to pay for myself. Whatever I thought about started to appear, even the simple things. I desired to have his name on a Pandora bracelet; a pillow made of us, dinner at a restaurant we were going to visit, and other things. I received them all. My friend would say, "Say it, Dan, because you are on a roll with God." I could imagine God saying, "Here you go. I know it hurts. I had to do it, but here's something to hold you over for now. I know you will love me regardless."

When Delmar passed, it was insurance-renewal time at his job. He let one of his policies decline so he could sign up for better insurance. He had just signed the papers before his death, so I was preparing to pay for his burial out of pocket. When I talked to the insurance company, they said he was fully covered because he correctly filled out the paperwork. The miracle is that he never made a payment! I was also able to cash in two policies. I had a dream three nights in a row that Delmar was handing me papers. After the third night, I opened a piece of mail similar to the ones that I had been filing in the drawer since 2006. This time, I decided to read it. I can remember seeing an amount of over $14,000. I was like, what is this? When I called, the broker asked my name and confirmed that there was over $14,000 waiting for me to claim. It turns out Delmar made an investment of $50 in 2006 and just forgot about it. Then I received another lump sum from another source.

What you don't understand is that *everything he prayed he could give me in life happened in his death.* It just proves that *not even death can cancel your prayer request.* God is going to honor His Word. Keep praying and putting your trust in God. Although I would give it all back to spend a day with him, I realized I had to keep pressing. God has not run out. He is perfect in thought. My only work was to trust God. Not only did He heal our bodies, but He saved me from anger, bitterness, violence, rejection, and destructive thought patterns. He became what I could be, loved me through it all, and patiently waited for me; I am grateful for that. The healing and freedom I have now are priceless. It took some time, but I needed it all. Now I know God as a comforter, healer, provider, way-maker, friend, my peace, joy, sustainer, mind-regulator, my song, the traffic controller of my life, my doctor, and advocate. He is my shield and the potter of my broken pieces; He's everything I need and He fights for me. I will never be the same Danielle I was before Delmar's death. My pain has become my power. My toolkit has been upgraded.

FROM THE OTHER SIDE OF THE BED

It was the first weekend in October of 2019. After countless nights of no sleep, I desperately needed a sleep solution. Frazzled and exhausted, I again took NyQuil to fall asleep. I rose early the next morning to attend a workshop when suddenly, I had a fainting episode. Fearing I would fatally injure myself in the bathroom, I managed to cut off the running shower and make a mad dash to the bedroom, but I didn't make it. I blacked out before reaching the bed. I woke up drenched in a cold sweat, with back pain from crashing into the bed's footboard, but I continued on my way. Then I noticed a rash on my hands. The rash consisted of red bumps and a little pain between my pointer finger and thumb, but that was the least of my worries.

Upon waking up the next morning, things had intensified. My body was covered with painful bumps, and that included my lips, mouth, throat, and face. On top of that, each time I had a bowel movement, I would faint on the commode. Although I'm a "figure it out yourself" chick, I thought it best to take a trip to the emergency room. I checked in, and they immediately put me in isolation. Several doctors and nurses came in to try to come up with some diagnosis. They narrowed it down to either mumps or chickenpox. Chickenpox won. I said, "Not the chicken pox!" They gave me an antibiotic and told me the symptoms should clear in three days. I then asked if I could take Ibuprofen to relieve the pain, and the doctor said, "Certainly."

Three days later, I was at death's door and unable to stay awake. After doing some research on the mix of the medicine administered and the approved Ibuprofen, I found out it was a cocktail for death. I was slipping into a coma.

After three days of experiencing fainting, spiking fevers, chills, panic attacks, inability to stay awake, dehydration from not being able to eat or drink from the painful mouth and throat blisters, and painful itching bumps on my body, I thought it was time to go back to the hospital. Still, I wanted to wait until my friend got off from work. I didn't want to infect anyone with what I had, especially my parents. While getting dressed to go to the hospital, I had another panic attack and this time I stopped breathing. I must have blacked out because when I became fully conscious, my mom was screaming, "James (my dad), she is not breathing!" I returned to the hospital with one foot in the grave. When I arrived, the doctors immediately forced three bags of fluid into my veins within an hour along with their most potent antibiotics because I was extremely dehydrated and my septic number was 35, which was supposed to be between 7 and 9. My heart was racing between 120 and 130 doing nothing. My temperature remained between 102 and 103 continuously. Caution papers covered my hospital door and everyone, including staff, had to suit up before entering my room. Strong pain meds, along with Benadryl, were given for comfort. They soon discovered that my kidneys were one point from failing. I developed a blood clot in my leg, a deep, constant cough, which caused me to lose my voice, and painful blisters from head to toe. Well, at least I knew at that point that it never was chickenpox but rather something life-threatening. After two days in the ER, they transferred me to a room on the renal floor.

I remained in the hospital for more than two weeks, drowning in fluid from the round-the-clock bags of antibiotics and other fluids. My limbs were enormous from all the fluid administered. I lost the use of my hands and became completely reliant on those who came to care for me to feed me, clean me, and attend to my basic needs. On top of that, it was my first wedding anniversary without Delmar. With the slightest movement, my heart rate would accelerate between 120 and 135 beats per minute. I could raise my bed, and the machines would alarm. I had at least five panic attacks, which almost took my life. I had a deep anxiety about the pain I was experiencing and the unknown.

I was sick, and they were losing me a little more every day. No one had answers. I took every test the hospital could offer, and still, there were no answers. I became angry as the days passed. Being poked every day for the five tubes of blood with no answers became very irritating. At this point, my skin began to shed like a snake. There was skin everywhere. Wherever I went, I left a pile of skin. I looked like a monster! I could see my family and a few friends as they looked over me with worry in their eyes. All I could do was look to heaven and say, "God help me!" How could I be in the right place with the wrong diagnosis? My life was in shambles, internally and externally. It looked like I would get my wish, escape the pain, and be at rest in the grave, and I didn't even care.

It wasn't until they told me my kidneys were failing and I saw the nurses dialyzing patients on that floor that I decided to get out of bed and live. I already had a port in my chest to draw blood because my veins had collapsed. Dialysis was my dealbreaker! I knew too much about dialysis to live a restricted life if I could help it. I felt as if I was a specialist in that area after watching Delmar's experience from the other side of the bed. I knew that disease like the back of my hand, and apparently, God was not going to let me die so I decided I was not going to live with a disability. I decided at that moment that I would live a healthy unrestricted lifestyle free of dialysis.

One morning, while lying in bed, an oncologist entered the room and alluded that they thought I might have leukemia and wanted to give me a bone marrow test. I'd had it! I said, "No!" and I decided to allow my spirit to heal me from that point. When you decide on what it is you want, every cell, nerve, and fiber of your being lines up to honor your decision. *A decision is power in motion.* You change before anything changes - which changes everything. There were some days when I would ask someone to pull the covers all the way up to my neck so I wouldn't be overcome by what I saw in order to hold on to the little faith I had. Don't allow it to become your excuse but your strength. Speak to that condition or thing and you tell it what to do! Your words create! Don't just think it, say it, and then start praising Him for the result in advance! Fight! Tell everyone what God is about to do. Make your confession in the present tense. Just believe! Don't become accustomed to the conditions of where you are. Have an optimistic outlook on your condition - and faith in God. I cried out again, "God help me!" and He did just that.

My kidneys started to normalize, and my temperature began to regulate. I forced myself to get out of bed and walk while panting for breath. I was determined to get out of that place. It wasn't until after discharge that I began to truly recover. It was touch-and-go for a while because of the massive amounts of fluids administered, which prohibited me from breathing properly. Everyone could not believe what they were seeing. They released me on a high-protein diet and plenty of liquids to regulate my kidney function.

My sister Denise was my ride home. There were four steps to climb to get into the house, which seemed like a thousand steps. By the time I finally reached the top of the stairs, I was lightheaded and completely winded. My brother-in-law quickly brought a rolling office chair to get me to the table to recover my strength. Eventually, I made it to the bedroom. My sister Denise, being a woman of faith, went and got the bottle of olive oil, anointed me, and prayed over me before leaving me in the care of my oldest sister Alicia. I could not lay flat or on my side, or I would have stopped breathing from all the fluid. I can remember trying to get out of bed, and suddenly,

I stopped breathing. I could hear my sister screaming, "Danielle, breathe!" with her eyes as big as silver dollars.

My breath started to return, and I slowly started to feel better. Although I was still looking like a monster and left piles of skin everywhere, God was healing me. Still suffocating in fluid with feet so large I could barely get a shoe on, I went to my PC. She mentioned I may have lupus. I said, "If another doctor tells me what I might have I'm going to scream!"

Those "mights" can cause anxiety if you let them. I was like, "Keep it a secret until you know!" I decided to believe that *what I had God had already healed*! I remembered those times when Delmar and I had to push through the illness. I knew that caving in to the illness only made it the boss, and that would prolong my healing. I had to speak over it and defy my feelings by doing what I didn't think I could do. I started making myself walk further and further. Every time I took a step, I said, "God, that's you!" He was there with me. He was doing internal and external work on me the whole time. George Mueller said, *"The stops of a good man are ordered by the Lord as well as his steps."* I realized that my life was under construction in more ways than I could imagine. God knew all of my patched-up areas of dysfunction. He wanted complete healing and freedom for me.

There are three levels we can address our pains: the problem level, the symptom level, or the root level. God was taking me to the root of everything I had ignored. My physical condition echoed my internal condition. In His way, He was answering my prayer. He wanted to work a permanent change in my thinking. God is not interested in fixing our symptoms (emotions and feelings in my case). He wants to get to our root causes and hindrances so we can soar. Many of us pray that God would relieve us from the symptoms or visible problems when there are internal issues. The Lord ordered my stop. The goal was never relief but wholeness and conversion. I knew I couldn't go on feeling the way I was not just about Delmar's passing but all the grief in my life. I was desperate for physical, emotional, and spiritual healing, and this "stop" was addressing every area.

Some of you may think it's the devil in a sickness, loss of a job, or sudden inconvenience, but sometimes it's God ordering a stop in your life. It's God allowing us to come to the end of ourselves in complete dependence on Him and His power and ability. It is not His will for us to live beneath our privilege. He wants us to be whole and to live abundantly in every area. Adversity is delivering development and opportunity. It is also God's mercy showing us a better way before destruction, but it's an indicator that something needs to change quickly. The problem serves as a check engine light. We receive healing, clarity, instruction, and a deeper connection with God and our purpose during these times. These stops can become the best starts in life.

Sometimes He allows multiple things to happen simultaneously, but He tailors your trouble for your strength. Sometimes it's multiple troubles in that trouble. He didn't stop the gossipers or the troublemakers while I was down. It felt that my problems intensified, but I can genuinely say I'm grateful for it all. It made me completely reliant on God to fight for me, and no one is an opponent to God's power. In my case, *what I left in prayer became just as important as what I gained.* God will allow some things to keep happening for us, not *to* us until it doesn't get a response. There is a lesson about ourselves that we need to learn from the pain. One day it will knock again, but you won't be there to open the door. Satan won't have a recliner to sit in your thoughts. You would have overcome it and adjusted to your new place of power. There is a liberating freedom when an old trick no longer works. Again, what we are not healed from will make a guest appearance in the future. I was carrying unnecessary weight and thoughts. I was in God's operating room.

Daily, I confessed that I was getting better. Daily I called on God's name for help. After a few months, I was able to attend church again. Still looking like a monster, I gave my testimony. It was the expertise of two seasoned nurses that diagnosed me. They quickly explained it was Steven Johnson's Syndrome. After doing research, I discovered that I had an extreme case of the syndrome. I had never heard of anything that resembled it.

According to the Mayo Clinic, Steven Johnson's Syndrome is a rare, serious skin and mucous membrane disorder that affects only one to two in a million. Often a reaction to medication or an infection creates a medical emergency. Flu-like symptoms appear first. A painful rash that spreads and blisters follow. Coughing, eye redness, itching, mouth ulcers, sensitivity to light, sore throat, or swelling are also symptoms. It requires special emergency treatment to eliminate the cause and control symptoms and complications. It was alarming for me because blisters covered my whole body. The trigger to my sickness (which was diagnosed as chickenpox) was the acetaminophen in the Nyquil and Ibuprofen. The cocktail prescribed by the doctor could have killed me at any time.

Shortly after this ordeal, I had an appointment with my oncologist. With a ghostly stare, he looked at me and said, "You were lucky!" I then shared photos of the ordeal. He agreed with the diagnosis and shared how rare it was. I'm just grateful to have survived. I have decided to make my life count by sharing my story with others.

Thank God for physical therapy. God allowed me to regain strength in my hands and restored everything that was threatened. My kidney function is normal, and my skin returned to normal ...with a few hidden blotches, and besides a little joint pain, I'm completely restored and grateful to be alive.

The month before this ordeal, I let my insurance lapse in pursuit of some cheaper insurance. It was burdensome to spend almost $1,000 a month on health insurance. You can only imagine the hefty doctor's bill from this ordeal. As I lay in the hospital, my mind started echoing, "Cha-ching, cha-ching, cha-ching!" I had to shut my mind down. I couldn't afford to think of how the bill was going to impact my life. I started telling people that someone would pay me for this ordeal and that my account would be paid in full. Have you ever had something so overwhelming happen that you didn't have the capacity to conceive the how? That was this hospital stay. Well, the bills began to roll in thousands of dollars at a time. Some were so outlandish, that all I could do was laugh. I couldn't believe that the doctors would put some of those bills in writing. Before it was all over, my bills were over $250,000. I was a widow, without the help of my husband, having to fend for myself facing a mountain, and I couldn't see over the top of it. I was it! I held to my confession, and when my faith strayed, my friend Watts would remind me of my confession. My faith was honored, and my medical bills were paid in full! As a matter of fact, the large hospital bill never came in the mail. He's a mighty God! God did not only take care of the entire bill but also the follow-up appointments, therapy, and everything else I needed concerning my health. Not only that but once again, I had insurance that paid off a credit card. The miracles that came from this situation changed my life forever.

I learned that the bed has many layers. The beautiful comforter, the warming blanket that keeps us warm, the high thread count sheets, the mattress cover, and then the mattress. The beautiful comforter is what we want to display and have everyone admire. We all want to be perceived as having it all together. The blanket below keeps us warm and makes us cozy in situations, even the ones that should have been gone. Then there are the sheets. Not many people know how to make up a bed. Those sheets are supposed to be so tight they can pop a quarter off them. Many of us have wrinkled sheets. They have spots on them and are in desperate need of change. Similarly, our lives are flawed, but we continue to climb into situations we know need change. Our sheets now carry an odor from all the dead skin (dead situations, circumstances, and relationships) that should have been wiped away. Then there is the mattress pad, which simply protects the mattress from parasites. I like to look at the mattress pad as grace and mercy. They keep protecting us from destruction and we take for granted that they always will. And then there is the mattress. The foundation of everything. This is about us. This is who God is after. He wants your foundation to be secure and built on truth. The mattress represents the foundation of your belief and trust system. When your mattress is worn out, it is impossible to get proper rest and without rest, there is no peace, just tossing and turning. The mission of satan is to steal, kill, and destroy. Once he has your peace, hopelessness, anxiety, and depression settle in leaving you with irrational thoughts and accusations. God wants to be your mattress or let's say, firm foundation. His truth will make you free, secure, and at peace. Let God make your bed properly and that was precisely what God was doing in my life.

THE PAYOFF OF PAIN

Fresh beginnings are often disguised as dead ends. Success is not the end of sorrow, but sometimes the beginning. OMG! I turned around, and the thing I feared for the last two decades had happened. I feared the day of his death and now it was my reality. It's real. He's gone! What am I to do with myself? I felt like someone handicapped trying to get used to life with missing limbs. What I relied on was now missing,

Have you ever had something tragic happen in your life? A cheating spouse, the death of a loved one, getting fired from a job, being evicted, an outrageous bill, abuse, or loss of a ministry. something that seemed to suck the very breath out of your body, something that you loved with your life. Hard blows can leave us perplexed and even confused. Zapped mentally, physically, and emotionally, we struggle to plot our next step and can't muster the energy to plan. Giving up seems to be the only option. The tragedy consumes our minds. For some, it takes days to come to terms with; for others, it takes months and years to decide to outlive the catastrophe. See, a part of us dies, and a part of us comes alive all at the same time. Henry Ford got it right. *The failure becomes our reinvention.* You're never starting over because you begin with experience. This perspective makes your mistakes training. God uses failure to humble and refine us. The obstacle is the way out! You can't solve a problem with the same mindset that created the problem. I dare you to laugh at your next failure, brush yourself off, apply the lesson, and keep moving forward. You're closer than ever to the finish line. With old crutches and the familiar snatched at once, we are between helpless and a fresh opportunity.

The truth is, if it were not for dead ends, we would not see the open road ahead and we would hinder our evolution. Bishop James F. Harris says, *"Trouble is fertilizer for growth."* So why do we have painful experiences? I'm glad you asked. It comes to make us aware, correct us, redirect, and teach us complete reliance on Jesus Christ. It also gives proof of your confession and reveals the truth about your belief system. It comes to direct us to a more efficient path. Without it, we will suffer from spiritual neuropathy. That is when you learn to operate dysfunctionally in pain until you become numb to what's going on and dead to the will and purpose of God, your dreams, and fulfillment. Trouble then comes to get your attention, to show you where you are cut, bleeding, and injured, to show you that you are in danger and need healing, and to make us pray.

Trouble doesn't always mean that you have done something wrong. It's quite the opposite. In the case of Job, the devil was not even looking for him. Satan set out to prove Job to be a phony, not knowing God suggested Job because he could trust the outcome. Yes, Job is the extreme case of losing everything including his family, and having a disease that consumed his body. But God trusted Job. Job himself didn't know his own strength. God had built him for this test. During his "downtime," he learned he had some underlying defects hindering his life. But know this: this light affliction won't last forever. In the end, when Job got out of bed, he realized that he had won, and God gave him double for his trouble. *Pain is inevitable, but suffering is optional.* It's impossible to live without some pain, but we suffer contingent on the significance we attach to the pain. Everything we encounter builds a story of hope; births something buried inside; and gives fresh vision to possibilities. Most importantly, it causes us to pull on God even more. You will recover! Romans 8:28 NKJV states, " And we know that all things work together for good to those who love God, to those who are the called according to *His* purpose." It's now time to turn your tragedy into triumph. It's now time to turn your pain into power. You may feel like you have been dealt a losing hand and everything you touch goes sour, but I have news for you: You can win with a losing hand! Remember, God has prayed that your faith fail you not!

It was during this near-death experience that I decided to live. Up until this point, I was in so much pain I welcomed death. All I wanted to do was escape. My true metamorphosis developed through my life's most painful blows. The pain was my alarm clock to wake me up to my potential and power. Until this point, I kept pushing the snooze button. It is not until we are forced to change that we change. I discovered that a few small things turned my pain into power for major payoffs.

- **Decide to Live!** Deciding means canceling all other choices. As stated before, pain is inevitable but suffering is optional. Everything is contingent on deciding. The power of choice is your superpower. I had turned my grief into an excuse to die. I had told grief all the secret recipes to my strength. I had started to give her the tools to destroy me. She almost convinced me of things that God never told me. My enemy was not Delmar's death but my dysfunctional thinking about his death. *The heart is the only place where we don't lie.* My heart was revealing my true belief system. Jeremiah 17:9 says, "The heart is deceitful above all things; it is exceedingly corrupt; who can know it?" The scripture is correct when it says it is the engine of everything we do, say, and think. My actions became the voice of my heart. Grief had me living as an imposter with words like never, always, why try, you can't, you will never, you're not good enough, you need more, you don't have enough or you are not enough, no one will support you, it will always be this way, you need more. Do these words sound familiar? I want you to imagine that you are an artist. You are the painter who gives significance to your pain and actions. Your reality today is the picture you've painted by your choices, not your conditions. It's time to reframe your pain. It's time to adopt a resilient mindset and crush your challenges. Your choice feeds the outcome. Refuse the avoidance behavior of finding excuses to play small and remaining a victim. To play victim means to refuse to go higher. I encourage you to consider evicting your inner critic. Ask God for a fresh wind to do your impossible and supersede everything you have done. It will take extraordinary faith, courage, and effort to break the habit of thinking small, but remember your why. If it is to be, then it's up to you. *Say it until you see it.* See it until you have it. Believe in your prayers and watch God come through.

What is your definition of living? Many people believe their dreams are impossible by the age of twenty-five; then they just exist until seventy-five for their grand exit. Yet, at their funeral, someone will stand over their lifeless body and say they lived a full life.

Living is more than existing. Living means:

- You have a mission for the breath granted every day.
- You have a cause and you live for an effect that you may never physically see with your naked eye, yet you continue to pursue the dream.
- You understand that your life is in demand and that there is a package only you can deliver.
- You have a vision that frustrates yet drives your everyday agenda.
- You constantly defy every limitation perceived for something greater.

- You have strong healthy relationships, personal growth and fulfillment, balance, gratitude, a thriving spiritual relationship, financial stability, and health.
- You fall in love with your uniqueness and God's design for your life with a sense of freedom to be uniquely you.

On the other hand, many exist. The existing do what's necessary to survive instead of thriving. Those who exist don't like the place they are in life, but fear and doubt have stolen the ability to take the required steps to achieve the life of their dreams. It is as if they are staring through the window of their souls watching life fly by, or they are living vicariously through others. A common trait for them is they can believe in others but have excused themselves from a prosperous lifestyle. *Refuse to settle into autopilot.* Take an active role in pursuing your goals and vision. Concentrate on what's evolving in your life. Revisit your goals and stay committed to the things that give you energy and joy. Refuse to be artificial by mimicking the lives and actions of others. Get back in touch with your maker and take the shortcut to a life of fulfillment and abundance. God had a plan for your life before you ever arrived. Catch up with His plan, promise, and provision for your life. Think about all the opportunities missed and forfeited, money, relationships, rest, happiness, and peace aborded because of your pain. You have wasted too much time already. Catch up! Get back in tune with His design for your life and soar.

Then, we need to hold to our faith. I had to trust someone far beyond me, and for me, that was Jesus Christ. I had to talk to God all day and dive even further into His Word, but this time not for knowledge but for the experience. Only God could save me. The Word hits differently when there is an immediate need. I had to trust His motives, process, and plan for my life. I had to trust what He had done, what He was doing, and what He was going to do. I started to apply what I knew and acted on it. In the process of being healed, I took the necessary actions to build myself up. When I came to an overwhelming point, I used His Word and told my situation how to behave. Moment by moment, struggle by struggle, He began to heal me and direct my footsteps. I had to remember that this was not the first seemingly impossible situation God had brought me out of. Everything I survived was necessary for my development. Take a moment now to reflect on what you have already overcome, the people and situations that seemed bigger than you. Look at you now. Let that be symbolic of the overcoming power within. Whatever your reason for not overcoming should be your reason to overcome. God was not the culprit of my suffering. I gave it power when I assigned its significance, but He allowed some things to happen for my growth, which was the key to healing. I'm reminded of an illustration God showed my dear friend Stanley Athey. The same muscles we see in a bodybuilder are inside each of us. The only difference is the bodybuilder chose to develop his or hers. *Trouble and pain are the gyms where we build our faith muscles.* We remain frail without them. As stated before, blame defers healing. We will never trust the one we blame. God is not the author of confusion; He is full of integrity. Sometimes, we don't seek His counsel and we walk contrary to the life He planned for us. But remember this: *the absence of God is chaos.* So, take responsibility for your choices, learn and apply the lessons, and stand stronger, wiser, and better, not bitter.

- **Discover:** It's funny how tragedy teaches us so many lessons. The teacher is in our pain. And if you're wondering where God is, remember the teacher is always quiet during the test. We ignore so many wonderful, buried gifts and equate them as insignificant until a challenge comes and forces us to use them. The pain produces the pressure to birth something new. Take the time to discover your gifts, talents, and strengths and develop them. Also, in your discoveries, take time to find and heal from any unresolved pain. You must show up as the highest version of yourself on your next level, or your hang-ups will trip you up and rob you of your success and fulfillment. Stop standing God up and show up for your healing and promotion.

  Finding your "why" or purpose for living is crucial to a fulfilling life. Reflecting on your values and what gives you energy can help you identify your passion, allowing you to focus your efforts on something that brings meaning to your life and those assigned to your life. Giving your pain an assignment can help you turn your struggles into a source of inspiration and provide motivation to help others going through similar challenges.

  Breaking down your goals into smaller attainable pieces will make them more manageable, increasing your chances of success. Always keep the finish line in the forefront of your mind. It's essential to consistently take action toward your healing and goals, no matter how small the steps may be. You can progress and achieve your objectives with direction, the right mindset, and consistent effort.
- **Detach** from limiting thoughts and toxic relationships. *Don't become secure in insecurity.* Joy awaits you! It may take a coach to take you back to the origin of your unconscious

pain, but the resulting freedom and peace are worth it. Isolate your pain by dealing with issues and painful experiences as they surface. Stop pursuing relationships that make you feel superior, that don't challenge your toxic behaviors, and stunt your growth. Don't play connect the dots with past pain. Stacking pain is a sign that you are not healed or let go of offense. Unforgiveness is an unsurrendered vulnerable access point for satan's control and manipulation. At his will, he uses the negative force of unforgiveness, baits his hook with twisted views and opinions, and goes fishing in your life for unresolved pain to control your thoughts, actions, and blessings. Without forgiveness, only trinkets of goodness come into your life, and your prayers are unanswered. Here's another fact: You are not forgiven if you don't forgive others. A stagnant, bitter, life full of regret is the reward of the one who refuses to forgive. Remember, God must be invited into your situation. To live in peace and abundance forgive even if that means being wrong to be right. Be quick to forgive and give the benefit of the doubt even if you must go home and wrestle with your ego and sense of justice. Stay free at all costs. Giving and accepting forgiveness is the mark of maturity, grace, and love. Forgive and refrain from the words 'always' and 'everyone.' It's not everybody and everything. In most cases, it's only one person. Decide you will live healed and have lasting meaningful relationships regardless of the pain you have experienced. The truth is we don't know what's in us until the pressure is applied. We must get light and unpack our lives. Unpack the weights, ways, past failures, bitterness, doubt, fears, sins, painful experiences, faulty thinking, setbacks, and other negative emotions and habits. Now that you know what your mental, emotional, physical, and spiritual kryptonite is you can now detach from your negative default behavior. In the words of Dr. James F. Harris, "God will bring you to it, but you have to kill it!" Remember, healing is a choice and you will have to play a part in gaining your freedom. Life will keep spitting us up at the point of our irresponsibility or in this case pain. In other words, *you will run into what you are running from until it is properly dealt with.* See it for what it is and release it! Just like in an airport, there is a weight limit for our baggage. Overweight baggage becomes expensive! When your life is packed to capacity with negative emotions and experiences, there is no room for the good stuff like miracles, revelation, power, peace, promotion, and other goodness vital for good living. Let the Word be your measuring stick, not the weakest link in your life. Pain can be contagious. Be careful not to share your pain with those who are already past their weight limits. Don't allow your pain to become the excuse to assassinate others to make yourself feel better. And by all means, stop borrowing other people's pain by claiming their baggage. The scripture says to cast all your cares on Him. Relationships are vital as you walk through life. *People are God's tool of choice.* The first inclination many Christians have is to distance themselves from the church when there is conflict, but it's crucial to remember that the church is God's idea. It's a hospital. As the potter molds clay on the wheel, God uses the church to shape and refine us.

In our daily lives, we often navigate, excuse, or even ignore conflicts and challenges in various areas, but when it comes to the church, withdrawing can play into Satan's strategy of isolation and stagnation. It's crucial to recognize that while the church may sometimes be a source of irritation, it is also a place for significant personal growth where the fruit of the spirit according to Galatians 5:22-26 can be developed. He sometimes allows people to stir us to see what's in us. Look deeper than the face of the pain. There's an echo there from something previous. *The current pain is only a flare-up of the actual injury.* People can produce the pain which produces the pressure, to produce the prize of becoming who God intended you to be.

As mentioned earlier, it's essential to seek support from others who can encourage, remind, listen, hold you accountable, speak the truth, check on your well-being, and pray for you when you are in acute pain. Three levels of relationships are crucial in any healing process. The first level consists of casual acquaintances with whom you share enjoyable activities. The second level is the inner circle, comprising people from the outer level who may have the potential to become closer or return to a more distant position. You may share a bit more with them, but there is no significant loss if the relationship doesn't progress. Finally, there is your core circle, which includes individuals with whom you can be truly vulnerable. They provide a safe, non-judgmental environment where you can express your true feelings and share your heart transparently. Above all, it's essential to find comfort in your own company.

Here's a bit of advice to stay free and a healing indicator. Can you:

- Love as if you've never been hurt.
- Give as if you've always been repaid.
- Forgive as if it never happened.
- Trust as if you've never been betrayed.

- Communicate as if understanding is guaranteed. (Always give the benefit of the doubt.)
- Persist as if success is inevitable.
- Try like you have never failed.
- Believe as if possibilities are endless..
- Grow as if learning has no limits.
- Live as if the next moment is your last.

- **Design:** Think about why you are in pain. What's the deeper meaning? Buddha says, "The moment you know how your suffering came to be, you are already on the path of release from it." Your questions are your answers. How is your toxic thinking serving you and what is its intention? *Fear is the source of most of our pain.* Fear is not real meaning we invest days, months, and years fretting over stuff that will never happen. For me, I had to take a moment to think about what I missed most about Delmar's absence and why. What caused my pain and sorrow? Yes, it is natural to grieve but where did all the other emotions come from? Pain is like an onion. The real issues are under the layers. Peeling back the layers causes us to cry. At a deeper look, I missed the way he loved me like no other. I missed his validation. I missed the security. I missed his companionship. At a deeper level, the pain was so intense because his love masked everything that was naturally lacking in my life, the areas I refused to acknowledge, heal from properly, or give voice to. It was a healthy relationship but I didn't realize until his death that I had a dysfunctional use for it. He had become a type of substitute god when it came to my pain. Who or what is your mini god or idol that you run to in times of trouble? Think about it. Are you hiding behind your children, job, family, generational curses and limitations, or even the church? Does losing the job hurt so badly because it became your identity? Does the inability to have children make you feel less of a woman? Are you afraid to move into a different realm of ministry or work because what you do is all you think you can do? Has your esteem plummeted because you are stuck in a ministry, group, or mission whose numbers don't reflect your dream or potential? Is your pain coming from the public embarrassment of having a child that is out of control because it tarnishes your image? *Pain comes when we ascribe the power and significance of who we are to what we do, who we belong to, or what we have.* Yes, we need to experience the results and feelings of success, but those results should never define our effectiveness and identity. We misappropriate blessings when they become our significance. This hurts to say but as beautiful and fulfilling as our love was, I used it as a bandaid or escape from my real issues. How was I going to mask my emotions and pain now? My role should have never been my excuse not to be all of who I was created to be. So often, we can make a positive action turn into a handicap. I hid behind my husband, church, and work. Good things - but I played small in my head and continued doing the comfortable things I could without much effort. I was busy but unproductive, ignoring the things that would build my muscles. I was essentially powerless. The pain was not going to ease up until it was dealt with and I found purpose in it and for it. I had to become vulnerable, allowing my weakness to be exposed to strength. I had to revisit my buried dreams, confront my insecurities, acknowledge and surrender my pain, seek help, and fearfully pursue my dreams. I allowed healing and faith to serve as my foundation.

Most people become depressed while searching for happiness. But success will not make you happy; rather, being happy will make you successful. When you can find significance in something that extends beyond you and becomes a service of joy, then you have found fulfillment. I pray that my story frees you and positions you to free others. That is the ultimate payoff for me. Smiles, strength, and progress become the payment of the assignment, which gives evidence of the power of your existence. It becomes the calling of your life. Be inwardly driven and allow your happiness to reflect on the outside. Will pain knock on your door again? Certainly, but the reward will trump the pain. I found that reacting differently was the only way to defy my fears. I was on trial. Don't allow the suggestions of satan to make you predictable in failure. Shock him with a godly response. I became clear on the end result and worked backward. I developed a plan with an inner determination to reach my goals. Allow the pain to propel you instead of paralyzing you. *Don't allow the pain to speak louder than your purpose.* Find your passion! Passion comes from the Latin word "pati," meaning "suffer." So what do you want that you are willing to suffer for gladly? Passion looks past the pain to see the vision even when you feel uncertain, terrified, unqualified, and sometimes even stupid. There is a reason why you were left here so make every day a day of purpose.

Take intentional purposeful mini steps: a class, a coach, software, a virtual assistant, a change in schedule, a meal plan, a vision board, a network to build relationships, or simply trusting God with your life. Pay the money, do the photoshoot, join a ministry, give others grace, purchase the equipment, get the license, and volunteer to try out opportunities. Or maybe it's something you need to stop doing. Maybe you need to cut down on your TV and recreational time to hone in on the project, cut your work hours, stop drinking or smoking, clear the clutter, change your company, or maybe just stop performing and be authentically you. You're not too old; your time is now. Turn that pain into power. But the first project is you. Write the vision and make it plain. Ask yourself, "Who do I need to be? What defines me? What do I need to let go of? How do I need to show up? What can I do now to accomplish my goals that will give me a taste of the results?" Pull those dreams off the back burner. Allow your talents and gifts to grow up. Refuse to spend the rest of your life in the lost and found, waiting for someone to claim you. Jesus has already done that! Get clear direction from your manufacturer, Jesus Christ. Direction and clarity shave off years of delay. Take advantage of opportunities. Tell yourself you can do it until you can't do it. Remember, it's never too late to be who you could have been.

- **Deliver:** Make up your mind to show up for yourself and others. You are necessary! Your life matters! You are at the right place at the right time. You are qualified for your destiny, which God created before your birth. Know your worth. Destiny has been waiting on you, and that tragedy was the vehicle. **Cancel every excuse.** Refuse to use physical pain pills that numb the pain like alcohol, drugs, sex, gambling, gossiping, people, shopping, overspending, overeating, isolation from others, social media, violence, and constant entertainment. I know that Delmar's death was a part of a masterful plan. He had completed his assignment of influencing thousands of people without social media and was tired. It was time for me to make my mark in this world. God took him in his prime. I became fearless! I had nothing to lose. The tables turned, and I

> started to bully my fears. I thrust myself into areas where I had always felt afraid or inadequate. I spent the money, gave the time, and practiced what I learned. I gave God my full trust and adopted who He said I was. The freedom I feel now is indescribable. I choose to live until I die. Execute your plan with passion and excellence. Get out of that fetal position and move to a position of power. Be specific and keep your plan in front of you. Trust God and His plan for your life; have faith in God and others. Put your purpose in an environment where it can grow. Disrupt your norm and give your passion oxygen to breathe. *Your past has evicted you, and your only option is to move forward.*

When you're in pain, sometimes you can't see the forest for the trees. Fighting through the brush, watching for poisonous and vicious animals, and battling brutal weather can steal its beauty. But just like God sustains the forest and supplies all of its needs He will sustain you. You can see the lovely trees, waterfalls, and beauty only when you can rise above it. Grief and pain can have the same effect. Don't try to understand everything upfront. Again, be ok with unanswered questions. Like the forest, at times it's a brutal journey to recovery. It's an ever-revealing process. Remember, our perspective is limited. It is limited to the moment we are in, but God has already been there, so He makes His decisions based on His design for your life. Soon, you will rise above it and find purpose in why it was allowed. God allowed Delmar to die with dignity. I know can see part of God's will unfolding. I'm ok not knowing all the whys. Either way, may this verse bring you comfort: Isaiah 26:3 MSG "People with their minds set on you, you keep completely whole, steady on their feet, because they keep at it and don't quit." I love how Romans 5:3-5 AMP puts it: "**3** And not only *this*, but [with joy] let us exult in our sufferings *and* rejoice in our hardships, knowing that hardship (distress, pressure, trouble) produces patient endurance; **4** and endurance, proven character (spiritual maturity); and proven character, hope *and* confident assurance [of eternal salvation]. **5** Such hope [in God's promises] never disappoints *us* because God's love has been abundantly poured out within our hearts through the Holy Spirit who was given to us." Again, simply trust His motives and love for you. There's a payday for your pain.

We are so complicated, but that's why we have a personal Savior that uniquely deals with each of us. As long as I had Delmar and his support, I was good. Being heard brought a sense of relief, but that was not healing. Once again, I was dealing with healing on the symptom level. Sometimes, as long as you have a little support, you continue to brush your problems under the rug. Support creates comfort; therefore, people seek others to validate their feelings. But it is essential to be truthful at all times. Agreeing with toxic behaviors can seal a person into wrongdoings.

The witness validates the feeling, and for some, this is the extent of their healing. But when we are in isolation with our feelings, it forces us to make life-changing decisions. Although Delmar always gave me the truth, his words still dulled the pain enough to cope. Are you coping to mask your pain? Coping numbs the pain and keeps you from what you really need. It can also form unhealthy addictions. It will still be there when the high wears off, and, most of the time, it will be joined by its cousin, guilt. The face-off between who you are and who you thought you were can be shockingly painful.

Ultimately, God wants our happiness to reflect from the inside out. Psalms 51:6 MSG puts it plainly, "What you're after is truth from the inside out. Enter me, then; conceive a new, true life." What we don't confront consumes us. Push the blame and shame away and own it so you can live free, pure, and transparent. You owe it to yourself and your loved ones to live your best life. There's something about being helpless that God can't ignore. Vulnerability is a must in healing. Become like a child in need of their parent's guidance to rescue them. I would only let God into the neat areas of my life, but God wanted access to every room of my heart even the messy areas. Delmar's death brought it all to the surface, and it wasn't going anywhere until I acknowledged it. I had to verbalize what it was, speak transparently about my feelings, and ask God to rid me of the harassing feelings. Some I had to pray about because something inside had justified those feelings repeatedly, but I soon recognized how they blocked my freedom.

The price was too high to keep it, and I couldn't afford it any longer. God slowly started to bring things to the surface, and I patiently waited for my prayers to carry them away. I asked my therapist why so many things were coming to the surface that had nothing to do with Delmar's death, and he gave me this scripture, "He won't put more on us than we can bear" (1 Corinthians 10:13). In other words, He won't just throw it all at you at once. He will slowly bring things to the surface when you are ready to deal with them and make some decisions. What a revelation for me! It just showed me how much God loved me.

We grieve what we do understand and what we don't. Again, Delmar's death was not the only grief in my life. My grief included some bad decisions, missed opportunities, allowing others to mistreat me, being silent, and tolerating things that I didn't like. In addition, I had sadness for making little time for the most important things, living for people who didn't love me, giving my attention to insignificant things, undermining my gifts, talents, and abilities, protecting people who assassinated my character and work, not taking that leap of faith and staying stuck.

You may be grieving staying in an unhealthy relationship, aborting a child, making mistakes in the past, missing an opportunity, forsaking your family, not taking time for what's important, breaking relationships, making bad choices, engaging in self-destructive behaviors, hurting those who loved you, and staying in a dead-end job. In addition, you may be grieved from making a bad investment, ignoring your greatness, not taking care of your health, suffering in silence, being insecure, not making a stand, ignoring your needs, or not trusting God. Regardless of what your grief is, it is real. It has the same impact, sorrow, and even guilt and can last longer than losing a loved one. You can't change the past, but what will you do with the rest of your life? *Your past knows nothing about your future. Only you can introduce them.* Be careful not to forecast pain regardless of how often an incident has happened. Will you allow the pain of loss and regret to stop you from living? If you only see it as a loss, then it's a tragedy because it has no meaning. It's not that you would ever desire for the pain to happen, but it's important to find the strength, significance, and purpose of what you will do with the situation in the aftermath. Dissociate yourself from it. Rise above it. Look down on it. What lessons can you gain from it? Let freedom become your new voice. Remember you are a new creature. Old things should not have power to rule your mind, body, soul, or spirit. Don't abort the mission of the pain.

Don't run from it. The pain is sending you a message. Ask God to reveal the purpose of the pain. Take responsibility for your part, whether you did something or you allowed something. Now, think about how you can use it to enhance your life and others' lives around you. Don't allow the pain to render you helpless. You have a second chance at life. Will you permit yourself to evolve without guilt? Living your best life brings honor to your deceased loved one and personal respect to your life. Respect who you are. What we hate in others, we want others to love in us, but now the ball is in your court. Make no excuses for stagnation. How will you live the rest of your life? If you're reading this book and still have breath in your body, you still have the potential and power to overturn the regret. There is an undiscovered power in your pain. Do what you know to do to have the expected result. Every time you overcome, you teach your past a lesson and defy a limitation. The intensity of the pain won't always last.

Maybe they died and you had unresolved issues or there were things you didn't have the opportunity to say. Hold a service, write a letter, visit their gravesite, put a chair in the middle of the room, and say everything you didn't have the opportunity to communicate. Most importantly, resolve beforehand that you are going to release the pain and the person once and for all. Choose forgiveness and live in freedom. Begin by saying, "This is what you did, and this is how it made me feel." Refuse to judge why and just release it. *If you let it go, it will let you go.* The only person you can control is yourself. Maintaining your heart is vital to your well-being. Don't allow your pain to prevent you from receiving love. Proverbs 4:23 NIV says. "Above all else, guard your heart, for everything you do flows from it." And if someone with whom you need to clear your heart is living, pray for the opportunity to share with them. When you have forgiven them, then you are ready for the conversation. The goal is peace, which means you could be right but take the role of being wrong to create an atmosphere of peace and comradery. This does not apply to abusive relationships. Then, set healthy boundaries. Note: if you are unhealthy while setting boundaries, your walls will keep in the bad and keep out the good.

You may ask, "Why must we endure such heartache?" C. S. Lewis wrote, *"Pain insists upon being attended to. God whispers to us in our pleasures, speaks in our conscience, but shouts in our pain. It is His megaphone to rouse a deaf world."* The average person cannot see pain as healing. What seems like destruction is often your advancement. *Sometimes, God's construction looks like destruction but He's building you.* Your life may feel like a strip down or house after a terrible hurricane, but some things need to be fixed that you have taped together (identity), some windows with holes (eyes), cracks in your foundation (belief), and other repairs that need to be attended to. What looks like a tragedy may lead to one of history's greatest spiritual triumphs. What looks like defeat may be turning into victory. What looks like suffering may be the harbinger of joy. So often, Remember, God will use something or someone you love to administer your needed healing. How else would He get your attention? That mate, child, family member, or coworker is not just acting up; they're ruffling those areas you refuse to deal with or need to grow in your life; the areas you keep trying to hide that taunt you privately. Those people are the leaves of the tree (symptom). God is after the seed that was planted (root). Until the root is plucked up there will always be problems and symptoms that continue to sprout up. Look past the face of the problem and into its purpose. Many keep missing promotions because of the vehicle of deliverance. We may not like the vehicle, but we will love the package it brings. Death was the vehicle for my and Delmar's healing. What a challenge for faith when God acts "like an enemy." It is then we must remember that despite whatever tragedy strikes us, God is not our enemy.

Refuse to get upset and don't let your mind become toxic with spiraling thoughts. Bad thoughts are like dust bunnies. They attract more dust until they become massive. When the dust settles, all you're left with is dirt. You may have to lose your job to enter the career of your dreams. That child may have to go to jail to become a leader in his community. You may have to endure sickness to overcome the fear of death, rejection to find your life partner, and depleted funds to create a multi-million-dollar business. Maybe that rejection was necessary for you to find like-minded people who won't hate on you but love and cheer for you. You may have to pay the fee as a reminder not to do it again. Hebrews 12:6 states, "The Lord chastens those He loves." What parent would stand by and watch their child make fatal decisions when they can intercede? Love always corrects.

Delmar's death sweetened Heaven's deal. I can now see God's purpose, and *purpose gives pain an assignment.* Face the worst, but expect the best. Reflection on our tragedies can offer us important insights and do much to restore hope. In a sermon, Dr. Russell Kopp stated, "He will always leave you with enough to start over and build even if it's only a foundation after a disaster." He is the God of enough. The widow in 2 Kings 4:1-7 was able to pay off her debts and was left with enough oil to live off the profits after she found a purpose for what she had and then made use of it. God can do more with your broken pieces than you could ever imagine.

Broken and contrite is a free passage for Him to move because the light can penetrate our darkness in our brokenness. So today, whatever you have been through or are going through, it won't last always. You're coming out. You will smile again. "Weeping may endure for the night, but joy cometh in the morning" Psalms 30:5b KJV. It won't always be like this. Tragedy will give birth to blessing; grief will give birth to joy. Continue to take inventory of your change. No one can overcome grief and pain and be the same. Capitalize on what's different. Allow yourself to evolve. What are you doing now that you didn't do before the situation, and how has your strength increased? What have you learned through the valley of affliction? You're going to need your now for your future. Each phase of your life is a stepping stone to the next level. Get up daily as a fresh, empty canvas and ask God to fill it. It is about surviving and finding energy and meaning in life while not forgetting. Who are you now? It's OK if you don't know what to do. Allow Him to direct your steps. You will know as you go! *It's your turn to live and shine.*

At some point, I had a vision of who I was, but I lost myself. Without goals, we latch on to people or allow our circumstances to influence who we are; after Delmar, my life changed forever. I will never be the same person.

Reach out for extra support during trigger times, such as holidays, birthdays, and anniversaries, and refuse to push away, judge, or suppress your emotions. Whatever we suppress intensifies. Intentionally stop and honor them. Again, you living your best life brings honor to their lives and yours. Keep the relationship fresh. You're not weird; you are just grieving. To keep Delmar's memory alive, I started a fund to build a hope center in his honor. My goal is to share hope and healing with all in my sphere of influence, and I am determined to take my husband where dialysis could not. Although his body is in the grave, his life lives on.

Meanwhile, I wrote this book as an extension of his life so that he could live forever and continue to help those facing medical challenges and those in excruciating pain desperate for hope. Writing this book brought me so much healing because I consciously had to think about Delmar and all the pain along my journey. I could better navigate the seemingly unbearable moments because I was constantly staying in touch with our memories and doing something. I promise that focusing your tears and pain toward a purpose will help you overcome, heal, and give significance to the pain. Invest in yourself. Put it all on the line. I invested just about everything I had in my buried dreams, and my future started to unveil. I desired to change that badly. *The proof of my desire was found in my pursuit.* With each investment and prayer, I faced and conquered another limiting belief. Every day I got up and said, "God, my life is a blank canvas. I give you complete control because I know you mean me well, and with you, all things are possible." Since then, my story has been featured in magazines, celebrity interviews, and podcasts and I have helped countless people navigate their loss and pain and find purpose. I am currently a life transformational coach who offers courses and challenges to help women and a few gentlemen reframe their pain, discover the pulse of their purpose, skyrocket their confidence, and cultivate resilient mindsets. It's rewarding to see others silence their inner bully, heal from pain, unleash their inner superpowers, turn their pain into power, and crush their challenges. When it's good, it's God. You too can rewrite your narrative. As a speaker, I enjoy seeing others experience the same freedom and understanding of their struggles and pain. Each time I share, I can measure my growth. I want to see individuals wake up to their power and purpose, where they no longer depend on the validation and opinions of others to know how amazing they are. They no longer dread getting out of bed to their mundane, painful life, unable to remember the last time they were truly happy. Their relationships are no longer crumbling around them and they are no longer frustrated and know what to do. In fact, their lives are no longer a prison without a physical cell but they now live a rewarding life on fire. My life is now a life raft for those in pain. I survived to help pull others through. Yes, I still have those moments when I just want Delmar and nothing else. Happiness has a different meaning since I don't have Delmar to celebrate my winnings. Success can seem dull at times without my guy. I still imagine what life would be like now, his opinion of current events, or cuddling on the couch to watch our favorite shows. God knows I miss making love. Still, I can now smile more than cry. I'm able to talk about him without crumbling. Every so often, I still scroll through my plethora of pictures and videos, and because I loved waking up to him saying, "Good morning, gorgeous!" I had pillow shams made with the saying on them. Even though it was challenging to muster the courage to move forward due to the guilt that threatened to surface, it was necessary. Somehow, I sensed a disconnect and felt as though I was betraying our memories, but in order to heal completely, I needed to let go gradually. My friend Stanley reassured me that Delmar would forever hold a place in my heart and in the chapters of our shared life, and that I was simply beginning a new chapter. What a beautiful thought.

Although I felt crushed and beyond repair, something inside of me screamed ONE MORE ROUND! When I wanted to give up, there was an inner determination to make my life count and to create a lineage for Delmar and myself. Right now, you are in the ring with thoughts trying to count you out and some trying to kill you, but it's not over. You have enough strength to win still. Although you may be staggering, get a good picture of life announcing you as the winner. Think of the movie *Rocky*. His opponent knocked him down with his face beaten and bruised and blurred eyesight. The crowd thought it was over, but he came back to win a victory despite the challenges, and you will too! This is how I made it, completely leaning on Jesus! His grace did the rest.

My dear friend, I understand that you may be facing one of the toughest battles of your life right now, and it's completely normal to feel lost, uncertain, and filled with doubt. But I want you to know that within you lies an incredible reservoir of power, love, knowledge, and strength, along with the support of those who care about you. Even when it seems impossible, you have what it takes to overcome this. As you stand at the threshold of your journey from pain to power, remember that within you lies an unyielding reservoir of strength, resilience, and untapped potential. Every trial you've faced, every obstacle you've overcome, and every moment of perseverance has sculpted you into a beacon of unwavering determination.

You will heal, recover, and rediscover your authentic brilliance. It's okay to feel the pain, and it's okay to shed tears. But despite the hardships, I urge you to gather the strength to keep moving forward. Embrace the transformative power of resilience as you rise from the ashes of adversity. Draw strength from your experiences, for they are the fertile soil from which your renewal blossoms for within you burns the fire of renewal and rebirth. You are not defined by the pain you've endured, but by the unyielding spirit that propels you forward. Even when you feel broken, remember there is a plan for your life, and you are being guided back to wholeness. Embrace the unfolding chapters of your life with purpose, fulfillment, and unconstrained joy. In the midst of your struggles, you are already winning, and one day, you will inspire others with the hope you carry within you.

I encourage you to hold on because this difficult time won't last forever. You are on the brink of becoming stronger than you ever thought possible. Keep hoping, striving, believing, and reaching for a brighter future. Hold onto your faith, and let it guide you through this storm. *Hold on to faith until it transforms your perspective from victim to victor.* Visualize the life you want to lead and hold onto that vision as you pray for it to become a reality.

It's important to let go of toxic thoughts and behaviors that weigh you down. Reach out for the support you need, whether it's through a support group, a therapist, a pastor, or your faith community. Most importantly, lean on your spiritual strength and trust that a brighter tomorrow is within reach. You are not alone and have the resilience to turn your pain into power. Hold on, and keep moving forward with love and strength. As you navigate the open doors and pathways that lay before you, know that each step promises new opportunities and personal growth. This is your invitation to transcend the boundaries of your past, to script a narrative of personal empowerment, self-discovery, and unyielding interchange.

Our victory is under warranty, and God is the guarantee. You have been left here for a purpose. We are all on Heaven's time clock, or should I say we all have an expiration date. It's not how long you live but how you fill the years. There is an assignment that only you can do. Don't waste this crisis! Someone left on the other side of pain needs your story of hope to recover. Remember, if you become a casualty, so will all those assigned to your life. It doesn't matter what others see in you if you don't see it for yourself. God revealed to me the name Global Girl over a decade ago. I adopted it not knowing the price. I even started a group called Global Girls Connect and now I'm here with a global message of healing and hope. I encourage you to *live every day with your obituary in mind.* Make your pain pay you! Do not merely exist—thrive, for you are destined for greatness. Walk boldly into the seasons of change, for the world eagerly awaits the brilliance of your transformation.

Yes, you will suffer for a short time. But after that, God will make everything right. He will make you strong. He will support you and keep you from falling. He is the God who gives all grace. He chose you to share in his glory in Christ. That glory will continue forever. 1 Peter 5:10 ERV

URGENT PLEA!

Thank you for reading my book! I pray that this book changes your life and that your pain is now your power.

Your feedback is vital to the success of this book and the spread of hope and healing, and I need your input on laser-focused solutions for those in pain.

Please take two minutes to leave me a helpful review along with your nuggets on Amazon letting me know your thoughts.

Forever Grateful,
Danielle Harris-Branch
www.DanielleHBranch.com

SPECIAL THANKS

As amazing as this book is, it was not done alone. Everything that is great is backed by people equally great.

To my Lord and Savior, Jesus Christ.

I am grateful to You for the love, spirit, strength, courage, healing, prayers, and patience that have shaped me into the person I am today. Thank you for entrusting me with this mission to glorify You and to spread hope and healing throughout the world. Your favor and endorsement in my life mean everything. I appreciate all the resources and support You have provided for my success. My life belongs to You, and I am dedicated to bringing You honor and making You proud. I love You, Lord!

To my parents and pastors, James F. and Sylvia H. Harris. Thank you for being the ultimate tag team of love, support, and faith. Your prayers, guidance, and unwavering belief in me have shaped me in ways I can't even begin to express. Your example has shown me that all things are possible, and the God I've seen in your lives has become my own. I couldn't have asked for better parents or pastors. Thank you for cheering me on and for seeing something special in me. I am truly blessed to be called your daughter.

To Alicia, E. Denise, Tione, my sisters and extended family. I am incredibly grateful for each of you and the unique ways you have shaped my life. Your unwavering support, guidance, and love have been a constant source of strength, especially during times of pain and difficulty. Whether it was coaching me through tough moments, physically caring for me when I couldn't do it for myself, or just listening, your presence has been a beacon of hope and comfort. Your love and care have been a tangible expression of family, and I am truly blessed to have each of you in my life.

To Frank Henry Wilson, my brother-in-law. Thank you for your selfless act of love in donating your kidney. I struggle to find the words to express my gratitude and appreciation. It was through your compassion and generosity that we were able to regain our lives, income, hope, and dreams. May you never run out of goodness and may God continue to bless each endeavor of your life.

To Takishia, my sister-friend, photographer, supporter, and human alarm clock. Thanks for believing and investing in my life and always being there regardless of the task. You're a true ride or die! Here's to many more adventures.

To Stanley, my dear friend. Thank you for never missing a Valentine's Day, death anniversary, or birthday since Delmar's passing. The heart-to-heart conversations have been priceless. You are a man of insight and a great friend.

To Darlene Fletcher, my mother-in-law. Thank you for your prayers and encouragement to keep pushing. I cherish our relationship. Most importantly, thank you for birthing my Pooh Bear.

To my church family, Redeemed Assembly of Jesus Christ. Thank you for being the holy squad that's always had my back. Your prayers, support, and reminders of my greatness are like treasures locked in the vault of my heart. You're not just a church family; you're an extension of love and support for which I'm incredibly grateful. Here's to many more years of miracles.

To my book tour guides Jack Canfield, Patty Aubery, Tamra Richardt, and Steve Harrison. To my editors Erin Leigh and Marion Sloetjes, and Wondering Words Media. Thank you all for your time, expertise, feedback, and support during this journey. Your creative ability turned my words and thoughts into a beautiful masterpiece. I could not have done this without you.

To my readers. From the bottom of my heart, I want to express my deepest gratitude for your continued support. Your enthusiasm for the book and your willingness to share its message will allow me to take my husband Delmar where dialysis would not allow him to go.

As you continue your journey, know that I am cheering you on as you migrate towards purpose, peace, healing, and freedom with joy and fulfillment. Your healing is my greatest payoff, and I am here for you every step of the way. Don't hesitate to reach out. Let's keep this incredible journey going together.

Made in the USA
Columbia, SC
01 March 2025

54564547R00098